SUSAN FARRELL

My
Homeplace
Inheritance

·THE·
BLACK
·STAFF·
PRESS

For my mother, Heather Georgina Maud Farrell,
26 April 1929 – 5 May 2020,
who gave me my love of cooking

First published in 2020 by Blackstaff Press
an imprint of Colourpoint Creative Ltd
Colourpoint House
Jubilee Business Park
21 Jubilee Road
Newtownards BT23 4YH

With the assistance of the Arts Council of Northern Ireland

LOTTERY FUNDED

Printed and bound by GPS Colour Graphics Ltd, Belfast

A CIP catalogue for this book is available from the British Library

ISBN 978 1 78073 262 6

www.blackstaffpress.com

Contents

Introduction

Mine is an inheritance of dreams and memories – of a crow falling down the chimney in the middle of the night, leaving me with a bad feeling about old cottages that has never quite gone away, even after sixty years. My childhood was the highest trees to climb, the sweetest apples to eat, the darkest streets to negotiate, and funny-shaped cars for a few and everyone else going to work on a bike. Where I grew up was more than a place or a country to me: it was a world. The type of world where friends went round in troops, where your business was your neighbours' business, where your misdemeanours might be shouted from the pulpit, where I would never dare to speak unless spoken to in an adult's presence, and where I had to do what I was told (unless I could definitely get away with something). Most of all, it was the world of frys, constant tea, bread and potatoes, melting butter and sugar crystals, crispy bacon rind, cabbage boiled to a paste and mushy peas once a week, coated in bacon fat, as many things were then.

My homeplace exists between the Blackwater River, the Bann River and the shores of Lough Neagh, a triangle of peat, fruit trees, mines, fish and subsistence farms until the late sixties when it was cleft asunder. By what? By the Troubles? By the depletion of its natural resources? The peat is still being dug and shipped across Europe, but there are no salmon left in the Blackwater, and the once glowing brick kilns are now dark, jutting out of the landscape like blackened, broken giants' teeth. Perhaps it is the onset of puberty that causes a child's perception of life to alter. Perhaps the magic and wonderment fades when the seriousness of life descends like a stage curtain, heavy and dark. Not entirely for me, thank God – my curtains are lace and there are still many openings into my Alice-in-Wonderland childhood. In my imagination I can still taste the cool well water, and smell the turf and the sizzling bacon on the cast-iron pan.

Although both my parents were brought up in this lovely part of the world, they moved to Portadown in 1953, three years before I was born, to a house supplied by Irwin's builders, the firm my dad was driving lorries for at the time. When I was due, they got a post-war emergency-housing prefab in Fitzroy Street. By now my dad was working for the General Post Office. I can still hear the thump of the nearby carpet factory's looms as they spewed out yards and yards of patterned wool carpet, and smell the cooking vegetables and fruit from the adjacent canning factory.

A child of the sixties, back and forth I went between the remains of the seemingly idyllic rural life of my country relatives, and the factory-heavy town. The rural relatives, at whose homes I spent so much of my time, had subsisted, even thrived, on their smallholdings until then – but a split in time was opening up. They tended their crops and their beasts, and then went to work at the brick factory or at Moygashel linen mills. The rural part of my life was the great adventure playground – searching for eggs in the henhouse, pumping water in the farmyard, and then sitting down at the oilcloth-covered kitchen table to drink as much hot tea as I wanted and to eat as many potatoes as I chose, usually served as a side to bacon or sausages or vegetable roll.

Sometime every May, a slice of County Armagh, close to the shores of the south of Lough Neagh, becomes pink with apple blossom. It is possible to get lost in this colour, its perfume, its magic. The line of the river between the Bann foot and Portadown, where I was born, is the eastern edge of this apple-growing area. I am very happy to have been a child of this county, and to have enjoyed many apple tarts in celebration of the fact. I love the giant Bramleys grown for cooking but that are sweet enough to eat raw. I buy them now from farmers who have set up stalls on the side of the road after the apple harvest. These apples are not sprayed to preserve them and for that reason taste to me like a kind of light, fluffy fruit cream that an angel might produce. Those with an even better flavour are the ones that hang over a hedge close to the road where you can stop your car and help yourself.

The orchards, the wide deep waters of the Blackwater and the Bann, the peat bogs sprinkled with white specks of bog cotton and the dying Victorian industries around Coalisland – this is my inheritance patch. I come from a line of subsistence farmers, big families fed off the frying pan who lived hard physical lives. Many of them are still around, proud and strong, a tribute to the land and lifestyle. I want to preserve and honour this life for, to me, it has much still to offer. Of course, there are the happy memories, and the way this old-style living has shaped me, but I also want to celebrate the simple things like walking everywhere, eating well, having fun, debating everything, being outside as much as possible, and growing food, then sharing it. I still do this – sharing home-produced honey, eggs and baking – and this book is my way of sharing memories and recipes of life at its healthiest and most fulfilling.

County Armagh Apple Tart

This is quite a difficult pastry to make but, as with all good food, it's worth persevering with. When you get it right, you will receive much praise. You could even enter it for the annual apple tart competition in Richill, a County Armagh village in the middle of the apple orchards.

At home, my mother made shortcrust pastry by using half the weight of plain flour in margarine or butter. There are many variations from different parts of the family. Aunt Sarah, who had been head cook in a big house, used butter. Serious bakers use half good-quality lard and half butter. Lard has a higher melting point than other fats and this produces a very good, biscuity crust. Other variations include adding cloves to the apple filling, my maternal grandmother's way of doing it.

Pastry
5oz (125g) butter
2oz (50g) caster sugar, plus a little extra for the top
1 egg, mixed with 1 tsp cold water
pinch of salt

pinch baking powder

8oz (200g) sieved plain flour

Filling

2 tbsp honey

County Armagh apples, about 2 large ones

Mix the butter, sugar and egg together with a wooden spoon until the texture is grainy – but the mixture does not need to be as soft as it would be for a Victoria sponge. Gradually incorporate the rest of the dry ingredients until the mix holds together well in a stiff paste.

Place the pastry in the fridge to rest – overnight is good; otherwise an hour or so will do.

When you are ready to finish the tart, preheat the oven to 230°C.

Peel your apples, slice them thinly and place them in cold water to prevent them going brown.

Cut the pastry in half – it will still feel quite grainy – and, on a floured surface, roll it out to fit a 12 inch (30cm) pie plate.

Drain the apple well and place the slices on top of the pastry. Drizzle with honey.

Roll out the pastry lid. With a pastry brush or your fingers paint cold water around the edge of the pastry on the plate. Place the lid on top of the apples, press it closed all around the edge and trim off any surplus. Prick the pastry all over with a fork and sprinkle with caster sugar.

Bake for 25–30 minutes. It will be ready when the pastry is a light, golden colour. Serve with fresh cream.

On Great-Granny Wylie's knee with Nanny Wylie and
my mother – four generations together in 1956.

1

Our Kitchen

Life starts in the kitchen. Ours was a prefab mod-cons affair, with a bottle-green-and-white electric cooker with mini Regency legs – resembling those of a fox terrier with arthritis – perched on a linoleum floor. To the right and beside the window was the Belfast sink – deep enough to bath a baby or the pet dog in, not usually at the same time – and a little wooden drainer. I remember my mother washing my dad's General Post Office navy canvas overalls in the sink with a scrubbing brush and washboard. No different from any other mother at the time, except the heavy canvas was stained with pitch, a sticky black coating used on telephone poles to stop the wood from rotting. Dad was a linesman, who shifted many telegraph poles on his shoulders, then climbed them to attach the telegraph wires. How did my mother manage to scrub off this messy stuff? I have no idea, but this heavyweight washing routine went some way to justifying our four meals a day and frequent frys.

Why I remember such small details I don't know, but I can tell you that the plug for the sink waste was made of brass, and hung from a brass chain anchored by the overflow and overseen by two hefty brass taps. In the corner of the sink was the only bit of plastic I remember – a triangular-shaped strainer into which the tea leaves were emptied from the teapot numerous times per day. The contents went into the garden compost pit at the end of the day, with the potato and vegetable peelings, to become compost for the vegetable patch the next year.

Our lives turned on this green enamel cooker and on the black cast-iron fry pan that sat permanently on the back ring, ready for action. This pan offered a sense of security. It offered fast food – faster and tastier than McDonalds – and you didn't need to be a TV chef to use it; you just needed to be half-sensible and have access to a corner shop that was always there, always open, and always had a bacon slicer and a side of bacon hanging from a meat hook over the counter.

The pan was covered with a thin layer of solidified fat that sealed in deposited flavour from bacon, sausages, vegetable roll, black pudding and the occasional bit of liver. It was never washed, for this would have destroyed the iron surface and caused food to stick on it. Worse than that, the valuable accumulated flavourings would have ended up down the sink. An occasional wipe was all that was required when the fat was drained off into a container. This is a hygienic system, as there are no bugs that will withstand the correct temperature of cooking fat. And bugs do not like high concentrations of fat, so the flavoured sediment was safe underneath, airtight and sterile. It meant too that even if you were only frying a slice of bread, the bread acquired the accumulated flavour.

The hot melted fat, or gravy as we knew it, was just

as delicious on boiled turnip, cabbage or mushy peas. Indeed, it was nearly compulsory – there would have been puzzled looks all around the table if it had not been offered at dinner time, when everyone's food was on their plates, and the best part of the meal remained on the pan. The gravy was like an elixir to us hungry children home from school, my dad who had usually worked outside all day and cycled to and from work, and my mother who had handwashed the laundry then put it through a mangle. My mother had an old nickel silver spoon reserved for portioning out the 'gravy', and an old china cup into which any leftover gravy was poured. The fat hardened and went white as it cooled down, and then went into the larder until the next time the frying pan was used, usually the next day. All chefs know that flavour exists in fat and that the best sauces are made by deglazing the fat and sediment from the pan.

A frying pan in the sixties was a frying pan for life and might well have been handed down from the previous generation. It certainly would have been a very welcome wedding present. A new one needed seasoning to seal it and to prevent food from sticking. If you buy a cast-iron pan and wish to re-enact the seasoning ceremony, simply cover the pan with a thick layer of salt and heat it. Turn the temperature down to low and leave it for fifteen minutes. Whip off the salt and the pan is then ready to use. Never wash it: simply drain off the fat when it is cooled into a suitable container then wipe the surface of the pan with kitchen towel. A good frying pan will be black as night as a natural non-stick carbon builds up over the years. Once it has created this surface, it's okay to give it an occasional slosh with hot soapy water. If you scrub it, the next fry will stick. If you have a disaster and you have no choice but to scrub it, then reseal with the salt and the surface can be re-established. You will have many frys to look forward to.

When anyone was hungry, all my mother had to do was heat up the white fat that was left there, then drop in a piece of bread or an egg or both – it was quicker than a microwave. Actually, you can fry nearly anything and we did, even sweet stuff, but using butter instead of lard. This is all that's required to live: the frying pan, a source of heat and half a pound of lard. You can use sunflower oil but it turns out that lard is better for us as it doesn't break down and has a higher cooking point so less fat is absorbed into the food.

The oven door was white with a dial thermostat to indicate when it reached the correct temperature. And the oven was well used, for my mother bought six pounds of flour per week to cover a big bake on Friday or Saturday morning and to make soda bread fresh every day. Soda bread is traditionally cooked on a griddle. We didn't have one, so my mother melted the lard that was in the pan, sieved it into a cup for later use, then washed and dried the pan, sprinkled it with flour and heated it up. The frying pan became the griddle.

My memories start when my eyeline was level with the thermostat on the oven. I guess I was following my mother around as, between the scrubbing of overalls and the baking, she spent a lot of time in the kitchen. As any child would, I learnt to hang around when the oven was on, attracted by the smell of the cakes or whatever was behind that door. 'Stay away from there, you'll get roasted!' No bother to me – I also learnt to wait patiently and get my reward for good behaviour, which was often a fresh bun or a piece of warm soda bread, dripping with butter. The next stage of development for me was standing on a chair scraping out the mixing bowl, wearing an apron longer than I was. Next, I moved on to rolling pastry or beating the cake batter. And I don't know anyone who can pass by a kitchen emitting a delicious smell and not hang around to see what's baking.

Beside the back door was a mini pantry. It was a built-in, floor-to-ceiling cupboard with metal mesh on the highest panel to assist ventilation. That small space held a surprising amount. On the top shelf there were tall cereal boxes. The second shelf held cups, saucers, dinner plates and cereal bowls, and the all-important sugar bowl. The middle shelf held baking ingredients, cans, the bread bin and the butter and cheese dishes. On the lower shelves were cake tins, tins of baked goods and our flask for summer picnics. At the weekend my dad's tin lunchbox waited there for Monday morning alongside budgie seed and other odd packages we didn't quite know where to store, such as the Christmas cake tin with its brown paper and string outer liner, shoved to the back with the jelly moulds and preserving pans.

I remember going back to get our mini pantry in my dad's car after we had been rehoused and the prefabs were being demolished. When we arrived, there the green pantry was, standing alone on the concrete slab foundation, strangely like the TARDIS, intact and as efficient as ever, ready to be strapped to the roof of the car. I remember thinking how strange it was to see the house lying on the ground in its prefab sections, and how easy it must have been to flatten our old home.

In our kitchen there was only one socket integrated into the cooker point. This worked fine as there was nothing to plug in except the top-loading washing machine: toast was done on the grill and the kettle was boiled on the cooker, needing supervision in case it boiled dry. Keeping an eye on the kettle didn't seem to be a bother then.

Our dining space was a fold-down table between the kitchen window and the pantry, around which four of us could sit. We could just about squeeze in a highchair as well. This area must have been designed by a man whose life experience had taught him that men were fed first and separately from the children, as often happened then. We rarely ate with our grandfather and when we did it was in silence. 'Chatty eating and messy children are for women' seemed to be written across his forehead. Of course, our table was never folded down – too much happened there. It would have been a great inconvenience to be constantly propping up the table, putting it down and then putting it back up five minutes later when a neighbour dropped in for a cup of tea. It was where the grocery box was sat when it arrived. And it was there we consulted the cookery books and rested the baking bowl as we took turns to cream the butter and sugar manually for the dozens of buns we made every week.

Change came when my mother decided she was going to buy a fridge. First, it had to be debated. Except for us children, whose role was certainly to be seen and not heard, everyone was involved in the discussions, including those who had never seen a fridge. This conversation started with the neighbours, and then went on to the family.

'Why do you need a fridge?'

'Where is the money coming from anyway?'

'*We* never needed a fridge.'

'It's only themuns in the States have fridges, sure what do they know?'

'What would you keep in it?'

'What's wrong with the press outside?'

'Oh, I had a cup of tea made with milk from Mary so-and-so's fridge. Wasn't right.'

'I'd say that wouldn't be good for you, eating cold stuff like thon.'

'Will that not put up the electric?'

My mother made the case for access to ice cubes (madness in my rural relatives' opinion, for there is nothing as cool as well water or fresh buttermilk) or treats for the children like ice lollies or ice cream.

'Sure, you'll ruin those childer with things like that – their teeth will be destroyed!'

I silently liked the idea of a fridge to be honest – fresh buttermilk was not a fun drink for me, especially when every other child in the street got lemonade. And then there was being told on a hot summer Saturday afternoon – hot enough for a treat because everyone is melting – that you can have ice cream. The jelly had been made and needed company, and a tin of peaches was to be opened. So off I was sent in my role as child message-fetcher to the nearest shop with a freezer, half a mile away, for half a block of ice cream.

'But Mum, it will melt!'

'Run! Here's the money – bring back the change.'

Imagine: imagine running with half a block of raspberry ripple ice cream that had been fetched from the bottom of a cavernous chest freezer in the corner shop, split in two (a whole block was more than we could afford), and covered on the open side with a bit of greaseproof paper. It immediately went into meltdown as soon as I left the ill-lit interior. In this particular shop, Whitten's, which provided both top-up shopping and knitting wool, a retired greyhound sat across the doorway for shade without caring about customers who had to step over him; sighing, for his racing days were over. Stirred by his memories of the track he got up, blinking, to see me off, running for all I was worth, then collapsed down again in the shade of the door. Would the ten ounces of milky sugar syrup survive the half-mile dash on the hottest day of the year? It did and it was worth it. I did the run many times.

But we were in Portadown now, not the country. We did not have access to fresh buttermilk, or a cool well, or a field full of strawberry plants or raspberry bushes. We knew how restorative these could be – on long Sunday summer afternoon hikes, finding wild raspberries to nibble was the best thing ever for thirst; or helping yourself to an apple from someone's orchard; or eating blackberries from the hedgerow in the autumn. I have adopted the same practice in my own garden – I work in it for hours in the summer, and have grown soft fruits like blackcurrants and gooseberries that I eat when I pass by with the lawn mower, wonderfully revitalising as well as thirst quenching. We were definitely not allowed lemonade – our morals as well as our teeth would be ruined – unless we made it ourselves. So the fridge arrived. It was white, with legs like the fox-terrier cooker, and took up more space than it deserved, with its two-and-a-half shelves, and an ice compartment barely big enough to contain a block of ice cream (which still had to be fetched).

Located in the upper-right-hand corner of this small space sat the ice tray, made of an unknown metal and with a removable twelve-section piece that formed half-square-inch ice cubes. My mother bravely tried to make ice lollies using orange squash and an ice lolly tray from Wellworths. We spent all day waiting and watching and dreaming about the home-made ice lollies. We opened the ice box door many times thus slowing down the process. Finally, on day two, my brother and sister and I sat round our table, hands clasped and eyes wide, waiting to receive this miracle.

After my mother spent some time trying to get the lolly out of the mean little plastic mould, one of us asked, 'What's wrong, Mummy?'

'They won't come out of their moulds.'

David started crying.

'I'll run them under the tap.'

We all sat and waited, and waited.

'Let me see, Mummy,' I said, expert on home-made ice lollies at the age of eight.

She gave us each a plate with the sad little orange squash lolly still encased in its plastic prison. We tried pulling on the wooden stick that should have just slid out with the orange ice. David's lolly came out in bits. He started crying again. It wasn't the loss of the lolly, it was the disappointment of the event. I felt this too but did not cry – I just dismissed the stupidity of the design of the moulds. We attacked the disappointment with teaspoons and butter knives and chipped out bits of icy mess, then licked our lips and wiped our orange mouths with the backs of our hands, then ran outside to play. We didn't ask for home-made lollies again, nor did my mother offer.

In the end we were more fascinated by the ice cube tray because we could help ourselves as long as we filled it up again and put it back to refreeze. Sucking ice cubes was a new occupation and involved inviting as many friends round as possible so that I could demonstrate the system and share the icy crunchiness.

We found storing the butter in the fridge was a mistake, for it went hard enough to make you cry. I still want instant soft butter on my bread and potatoes. Cheese tastes better at room temperature so it stayed in the larder. But we liked the way jelly could be set in a short time. And the way the milk kept cool. It was better for ham and bacon too, and saved many daily runs to the shop. I imagine I got a little plumper. What was left in the fridge apart from ice cubes? Probably the milk. Even if we bought meat and put it in the fridge it was still eaten on the same day. The fridge novelty soon wore off. We carried on much as before.

Perhaps my grandparents' generation were right after all about fridges. A chicken's neck could be wrung on a Sunday morning for Sunday lunch, so what's the problem? And for each day fruit or vegetables are stored, their vitamin content diminishes. Compare for yourself the taste of a raspberry, tomato or anything raw and fresh for that matter just picked out of the garden to that just picked out of a fridge. The fresh warm fruit is juicy and sweet but the cool refrigerated fruit is dull. Bigger houses would have had larders with a slab bench made of a cool stone like granite or marble that never warmed up, where they kept the cheese, butter, cream, bacon and cold meats. Some households without this facility might have had a food safe. This was a small aerated press on long legs. Its sides and front panels were made of either finely woven mesh wire or sheets of aluminium with finely punched holes. It was situated in a shady place outside and could be mistaken for a weather station. It kept the sausages cool for the evening meal or protected the setting jelly, perhaps made as a treat for visitors.

I still mistrust stored 'fresh' food that is more than twenty-four hours old. I understand how refrigeration works. It keeps the bugs dormant and extends the life of the wonderful choice of fruit, vegetable, dairy and deli foods we have on offer today, but fresh garden produce at its natural outdoor temperature tastes better, especially in summer. If my ancient rural relatives were brought back down to earth for a tour around a Tesco store, it would

11

seem like an Aladdin's cave to them. They would be highly entertained, amused and have enough material for debates and arguments to see them through eternity.

A Fry

Walk around any street here in my childhood at almost any time of day or night and you will likely smell bacon frying on a pan – an aroma so enticing and so evocative of comfort and delicious Irish cooking. I still 'get the pan out' to fry on a regular basis. My fry consists of sausages, bacon, egg and potato bread. As a nod to the five-a-day rule, I may include mushrooms, courgettes and peppers. My favourite additions are fried Bramley apples or cabbage as I am almost always having a fry for lunch or an evening meal. We were never served a fry at home for breakfast the way it is in hotels. Our traditional breakfast would have been porridge.

No cookery books that I know give instructions on how to prepare the most important meal known to Western civilisation. The skills required come from our genes and from observing and absorbing them in the Irish home. A good fry is actually quite difficult to achieve. The bacon needs to be crisp, the egg needs to be plump, spotless, and neither too hard nor too soft, and no one wants any of the individual elements of their favourite meal to be swimming in fat. Domestic science at school did not cover the correct way to cook with fat – a great oversight as that was how everyone cooked – but the classes did emphasise how to identify good-quality fresh ingredients, and the necessary role fat played in our diet. It is the only source of vitamins A, D and E, which are fat-soluble vitamins. So you can see why a traditional fry is actually a very important part of our dietary intake. Apart from food values, in 1967 we were taught that fat provides essential satiety.

Ingredients

Bacon
Bacon with too much added water will lower the temperature of the fat and instead of a crisp rasher you will end up with something that looks like shrunken pieces of boiled ham. Traditionally cured bacon is dry, doesn't shrink when cooked and is crisp when fried. There were many fights in our house over who got the crispy rind – when you get the quality and cooking just right, crispy fried rind is as sweet as honey.

Sausages
All frys in my childhood included beef sausages. When I first came across pork sausages, I thought they looked and tasted peculiar. Somehow the world has reversed since then. In Northern Ireland there are a number of butchers reviving the beef sausage, using traditional recipes and sometimes also traditional breeds of cattle, such as Irish Moily. Meat from these breeds has a noticeably better flavour, so they are definitely worth searching out. It's also important to make sure that your sausages have a high meat content, otherwise they will spit hot fat and shrink.

Vegetable Roll

Vegetable roll is like a large pink sausage flecked with green, about two-and-a-half inches in diameter, that comes in a plastic tube. The butcher simply cuts off the number of slices that you want. It's slightly spicy, and is a succulent and tasty addition to the fry. The greenery, like the name, is a mystery, for vegetable roll is at least 99.9 per cent animal content and rusk.

Black Pudding

There is something primitive about black pudding. It seems to wake up my ancestor genes. After I have eaten it, I feel as though I hunted and caught what I just ate when in fact I've only been to the butchers and bought some pudding for a change. It's not for the squeamish but the blood content is a valid and tasty source of protein. Like the sausage, there are many variations across the world, for blood as a source of food is too good to waste. There is a variation in Ireland called white pudding, bloodless mind you, but maybe more suitable for the uninitiated. A good pudding, black or white, is packed with barley grains and quite spicy. Blood has a smoky flavour, but get over the blood thing – there is blood in meat, and it contains iron, essential for health. One slice is usually enough; one slice of black and one slice of white is a treat.

Eggs

One or two? Soft or hard? Personally, I like mine soft in the middle and crisp around the edges. An egg can only be perfect if it is fresh. If your egg runs all over the pan when you crack it in, scrape it straight into the compost bin because it is stale. The yolk and inner white should be domed and gelatinous. If you aren't sure how old your egg is, drop it gently into a jug of water. If it floats, it isn't fresh; if it sinks, your fried egg should be perfect. For an even more perfect egg, get your own hens.

Breads

Traditionally, soda farls and potato bread are served with an Ulster Fry. Usually I would cook these at the end, for then they will absorb some of the flavour of the previously fried ingredients. Wheaten is good too, as are most breads. The secret to frying bread is that the frying medium must be good and hot (see below), and not old. Lard or bacon fat can be reused for frying, but it's less advisable to fry in old oil. The chemical structure breaks down after a very short time and soaks into any bread, making efforts at fried bread a soggy mess. Fried bread should be crisp and brown on the outside and soft and hot inside, without a hint of grease.

The Frying

If you would like to get a fry right, then bear with me on the technical stuff. All fats have a melt point, a smoke point, and flash point. Fat that has just melted is too cool for a fry. The smoke point is a warning that the fat is too hot – the ingredients will burn on the the the outside and stay raw in the middle. The next level up is flash point – when flames start dancing on the surface of the oil.

The correct cooking temperature creates crispness –

the ingredients will seal quickly and not soak up the fat. If the temperature is correct, you will end up with more fat in the pan than you started with. A correct frying temperature is between 175°C and 195°C, indicated by a slight haze rising from the fat or oil. You need to try to maintain an even temperature. You will definitely need to cook your fry in batches, so as you remove one batch of sausages from the pan to a low oven to keep warm, the temperature of the fat or oil in the pan needs a couple of minutes to come back up. Start with the heavier, denser items like sausages and black pudding, and keep these warm in the oven, then continue with the lighter ingredients. A good fry happens quickly and therefore requires continuous attention.

To shallow fry an egg, your chosen fat should be clean (strain any previously used fat or use fresh fat, or fresh oil if you prefer) and giving off a heat haze. Have a spatula and a warm plate ready. Crack the shell with a sharp knife and gently drop the egg into the fat. A shallow frying medium will not cover the yolk, so tip the pan slightly and using the spatula, direct some of the hot fat over the egg until the white is opaque. You now have to decide if you want the egg to be soft or hard in the middle. All of the white should be opaque at whatever stage you decide to lift the egg out onto the warm plate. Eggs coming out of the fridge will lower the cooking temperature of the fat or oil, so they are best stored at room temperature.

If I am frying potatoes, I will use an additional pan as these take longer to crisp up and reheat than, say, something like cabbage. As lots of your ingredients are coming out of the fridge, the temperature of whatever cooking medium you use is lowered momentarily until the food heats up. This does interfere with the end result, causing a reduction in crispiness or causing some foods to go soggy. In an ideal world we would still be using larders, but the best alternative is to take your fry ingredients out of the fridge a couple of hours before you intend to fry them (obviously, do not leave them sweating somewhere too warm). Or go back in time to 1960s Ulster, get what you need on the day and don't refrigerate it.

2

The Smallholding Family

Drumnaspil is a townland of Tamlaghmore in the parish of Killyman in the barony of Dungannon Middle. In the 1911 census, there were only seven farms in the townland, one belonging to my maternal grandmother's family, the McKays. The census listed my great-grandparents, Francis (59) and Margaret (45), along with ten children. Francis was to die before their eleventh and youngest child Lila was born. Susan (Nanny Wylie), my grandmother and namesake, was then ten. She would have four more years at school before she was off to work. Her sister, my Great-Aunt Sarah, was already out working in domestic service. She remained at the farm – the homeplace – until the 1970s, with her brother, Frank, who also never married.

At the time of the census, there was enough land to feed pre-work youngsters, and enough to share with the neighbours when times were tough. Granny McKay had been known to wring a chicken's neck to make sure her neighbours' children did not go hungry. But every one of her eleven children went out to work so that they could contribute to the household income. The children who married would get their own places – not with cows and hens so much, but in workers' houses attached to mills or in the new public housing schemes being constructed to replace the mud-walled, whitewashed cabins so synonymous with the Irish landscape at that time but already romantically degenerating into unsuitability for habitation.

In the adjoining townland of Drumenagh were eleven Farrells, including Charles, my paternal grandfather. He would go on to marry my paternal grandmother Minnie, also from a neighbouring family. The Farrells had a bigger, grander farm than the McKays and contributed to the local economy as suppliers of milk over and above just feeding themselves. Like everyone else, their cows, hens, potatoes and vegetables from their fields fed the family.

All these twenty-two McKay and Farrell children survived into adulthood. My paternal and maternal grandparents lived well into old age, as did most of their siblings, Nanny Wylie making it to 104 and without any real health issues. A testament to their food and lifestyle? Something worth considering. Certainly the way they lived seems to have worked for Minnie who – as a young woman, before she married Charles and became my Granny Farrell – went from flu house to flu house near the area now known as Laghey Corner. It was the great flu epidemic of 1918 and she was twenty. More devastating than the plague or the First World War in terms of numbers of casualties, it had come to Ireland and to that wee boggy patch between the Bann foot and the Blackwater River, our family's home patch. Perhaps it was carried on a coal barge that had travelled up from Dublin to be restocked; perhaps it came with First World War veterans, glad to be home after the horrors they had witnessed, only to find that the Spanish flu had come with them. The numerous branch lines of the railways at that time, like capillaries in a human body, allowed the virus to find its way into every nook and cranny of rural Ireland as the soldiers travelled home and unknowingly took it right in through their families' always-open doors. One of the reasons for this flu being so devastating, apart from the lack of understanding of viruses and the fact that antibiotics hadn't been discovered, was rural poverty: poor diets, poor housing and no health service. The flu affected all levels of society, but poor rural families suffered the most.

Tall, lean, twenty-year-old Minnie went from neighbour's house to neighbour's house to nurse the sick and dying. What did she do there? We can only imagine as there was nothing for fever except cold compresses, maybe aspirin. There were plenty of concoctions on the market, but no one really had a clue what might help. She may have mopped brows; she may have changed bed linen and washed it in a tub, then hung it outside in the orchard for the wind to billow and blow the germs away.

Whatever that young woman was made of, she survived constant contact with the virus, walking for miles to neighbours' cottages, and spending many long days nursing whoever needed help.

After the flu pandemic had passed, my grandmother went on to have eleven children – including my dad, now ninety-five – most of them weighing in at birth at between eleven and twelve pounds. A strong woman indeed, responsible for some of my genes and attitudes, and survival skills. My Granny Farrell was a legend in her own time, a hero to my mother, who talked frequently about the birth weight of my dad's siblings. When one of us from the younger generation had a baby she always reminded us of what my granny had been made of by saying, 'And there were twins as well!' My memory of Granny Farrell in her late eighties is of a straight-up-and-down elderly lady with the same long hair she'd had all her life plaited and wound round her head, kirby gripped in several places. Always ready for action – possibly the arrival of a squad of grandchildren requiring bread and jam and tea – she wore a wrap-around apron and sat at the table with her bony hands on her lap keeping an eye to the kettle on the range.

Go back to Tyrone in the 1920s and 1930s, where my parents grew up, and have a look around. It is part bog, part farmland, in the flood plain of the Blackwater River. It is scattered with one-storey, whitewashed, thatched stone cottages, gleaming in the sunlight, for lime wash contains the crushed remains of shells and their iridescence is still active. Constant turf smoke belches out of all the chimneys from perpetual fires. Turf blocks are stacked up against a side wall, enough for the winter. Hens scratch about in the yard. There may be a leg of bacon smoking in the chimney, the slow drift of turf smoke drying it and curing it, or so I am told by my dad. He and his friends and brothers and sister went to Mrs Murphy's céilí house, one of the little cottages, on a Saturday evening for their

Aunt Ivy, my dad's sister, at Granny Farrell's house in Cohannon in County Tyrone. Granny Farrell is a shadow in the doorway. How do I know it's her? This is the way she habitually stood.

entertainment. A big black cast-iron crock of porridge simmered over the cottage's turf fire for supper. These fireplaces were big enough for an average person to stand in, for the fire was the cooking place. One winter evening my dad was given the job of fetching the porridge pot to the table. Fascinated by the fact that he could see the sky by looking up the chimney, he got caught in the act as a flurry of snow fell. Knowing my kin as I do, them seeing my dad covered in snow would have been the best laugh of the evening.

Everyone in my dad's neighbourhood had hens and likely a goat or a cow for milk and dairy. Everyone grew potatoes. This was their basic daily fare: potatoes, milk and eggs. After the slaughter man had visited, the neighbour with the pigs then shared the offal around the locals, so you might have pig's liver with your potatoes and butter that evening. This was a regular occurrence in my father's life, something to look forward to. He regarded it as an enjoyable neighbourhood event. Liver was a good food for those on a low meat diet – it provided iron – and is very delicious fried with bacon and served with potatoes and cabbage on the side.

Big families were commonplace – to have ten-plus children was not unusual and no bother, for it was all help around the farm. Cleaning out the byres and pigsties were daily duties as were checking livestock and collecting eggs. All good jobs for children. Better-off homeplaces would have a hayshed, a barn, a pigsty and a chicken house, and a dairy arranged around a central yard with a pump in the middle. The pump was not just for this farm, it was for the neighbourhood, and locals got their milk, butter and buttermilk here as well. One of my dad's jobs as a child was to collect butter and buttermilk. On a hot day, going to collect butter, he says he was often given a drink of cold buttermilk straight out of the churn to quench his thirst.

My parents' families were neighbours in adjoining labourers' cottages in Tamnamore; they worked and socialised together. Each cottage had enough of a plot to feed the family for a year with potatoes, cabbages, carrots, beetroot and turnips. All these root vegetables were stored for use through the winter. Setting the family up for the year also included the turfcutting when all hands were on deck. Their turf patch may have been handy – just over the back fence – but cutting sufficient turf for a year is a major calorie-burning, back-breaking undertaking. The many tonnes needed for the homeplace fire on which my grandmother cooked all the food for the family, boiled all the water they needed and which heated the house add up to something worth thinking about. So, unless you couldn't walk, you were in the peat moss; if not cutting, then stacking, or bringing the tea and soda bread for the lunch. Not just a family affair, this was a cooperative effort with the neighbours, as were all smallholder tasks.

At one time, the Blackwater River was full of salmon. My mother's father, Granda Wylie, had fishing rights from the MacGeough-Bond family whose estate, the Argory (now a National Trust property), ran alongside the river. This meant he could catch salmon by stretching a net across the river. The salmon simply swam into the trap on their migration upstream. What a shock for these magnificent beasts to be halted in their mission. They were heavyweights – three foot long or more – and with Trew and Moy station only a mile away, the salmon from Granda's nets could be on a plate in the dining room of the Great Northern Hotel in Belfast in the evening. This was a living for my grandfather, who was a subsistence labourer, and the sale of the salmon fed my mother, aunt, uncle and grandmother in the thirties. This was a time of depression, pre-welfare state, when there was no income support or unemployment benefits and no health service. Once when my dad called round to visit my mum before they were married they all ended up out on a boat on the Blackwater River to help Granda Wylie haul in his nets. My mother complained about these sorts of chores for many years, long into her later life. To me it sounds like fun, but then I didn't have to do it. However, I did get taken out on mushroom-picking expeditions with Granda Wylie and got a flavour of what that life might have been like – we went to pick the mushrooms because they were free but also because fresh juicy horse mushrooms are the most incredibly delicious things to have on your dinner plate.

My mother enjoyed the company of my dad's sisters, who lived next door, and going out to work in Moygashel linen mill. In 1942, aged fourteen, my mother had joined the hundreds of girls streaming into the mills first thing in the morning, pushing and shoving to get clocked in before their start time.

To support his family, my maternal grandfather, Granda Wylie, grew vegetables in the front garden, the side garden and the back garden of their cottage. Even when my mother and sister went out to work in Moygashel and brought in vital money, he continued as a market gardener for this was his thing. Every weekend he took a cartload of vegetables to Portadown to sell. Their house is still there, the last of the three labourers' cottages on the Bovean Road where it meets the Tamnamore Road, adjacent to the Blackwater River and a couple of miles from Maghery where the Blackwater pours into Lough Neagh. It has a long, narrow, triangular garden, which is grassed over now but which was stuffed with vegetables when the Wylies were there.

Cabbage was one of their staples. There is a variety of cabbage that grows to about three-foot high or more, and its stalk is as hard as wood. Granda Wylie grew these in his front garden. A multipurpose vegetable: a neighbour on his way home from a bevy could stop and lean on the cabbage for a rest, relight his pipe and then have a go at getting the rest of the way up the road to his home.

A true gardener, Granda Wylie loved to experiment with exotic plants. One year he put sweetcorn in. Each day he watered it and tended it. The family watched, anticipating the grand event that was to come: fresh corn on the cob, straight from the garden and as sweet as honey, dripping with home-made butter. The source of the butter was looking on. She flicked her tail and munched the grass in the next-door field; head down, keeping her thoughts to herself, but occasionally swivelling her big brown eyes towards the vegetable patch. Towards the end of the summer, when the vegetables were at their peak – the runner beans were a foot long, and everyone was sick of giant cabbage – my grandmother went early with the bucket to milk Nellie. Instead of finding her in the field, there she was in the vegetable patch, finishing off her breakfast of corn on the cob. My grandmother was a person who knew how to deal with injustice, and I imagine that that big old beast got a mighty whack on the arse on her way back to the field. Cabbage again for dinner.

Halfway between this homeplace where my mother lived and my Nanny Wylie's homeplace at Ballnakilly was the local grocer, Henderson's, next to Tamnamore Public Elementary School. Handy for Dad because he and his siblings got a penny each on the way to school every day to buy a Paris bun for lunch. While Nanny Wylie made soda bread every day for the eleven children in Dad's family, it is unlikely that there would have been time to bake home-made bread every day.

My mother's abiding memory of the Farrell family at home on a Sunday afternoon when she and my father were courting is of Granny Farrell sitting at the kitchen table with several batch loaves. As the various waves of family and friends arrived, she simply kept slicing bread for bread and jam, and handing out pieces (the Scots word for a sandwich). Most were returning from the compulsory Sunday afternoon three-hour hike, kitted out in the latest styles purchased from their earnings in Moygashel mill. As Granny Farrell started a new round of slicing, someone would go to the range and make a fresh pot of tea from the always boiling kettle.

They'd all have spent the Saturday night before at either a céilí house nearby or playing darts at home. The big pot of porridge simmering on the range for everyone's supper, whatever the venue, ended the evening, usually very late and fuelled them for the walk home. This was the weekend.

The young gang of Farrells and Wylies and their neighbours did the farm tasks in the evening, once they were home from work. The main job in the summer was haymaking, not only your family's but everybody's. June was a month of working in the factory then cutting hay in the evening, unless it was raining. No one remembers the rain, though – they just remember the long, long June days, light enough to work until eleven at night. If they found this exhausting – a day in a factory and then an evening in the hay field – no one ever complained. Weekends became filled with the hay-cutting: the cutting, turning it so that it dried, the staying out until it was all done and everyone's hay was in.

The meal on the hayfield was soda bread and butter, maybe cold potatoes from the night before, and cold, cold, thirst-quenching buttermilk. A good time was always had, a chance to carry on with your friends, and a potential bonus was discovering mini honeycombs built by a breed of bee that operates on its own and has its stores in the ground. The hay-cutting lads and lassies treated these finds like sweets – they ate the honey, wax and grubs and all.

Back at the house, if they were still thirsty, and I imagine that after spending a hot day in a hayfield they must have been, there was an enamel bucket full of home-made beer or buttermilk, or thinned-down milk.

Aunt Ivy (left) with Mummy's sister, Aunt Lynn, and their neighbour, John Hodgett.

Granny Farrell would boil a big pot of spuds, in those days a stone weight (well over six kilos) at least. Thirteen people around a table hungry from burning calories in a hayfield are fit for a stack of potatoes – skins still on, for who would peel this number of potatoes? – and butter. In some houses the boiled spuds were simply piled on to the table, in a mound nearly as big as the haystacks the workers had just made in the fields. A skilled eater of unpeeled spuds has to be able to hold the hot potato in one hand and with the other remove the skin with a knife – a tricky and burny job. Good-quality potatoes of the type favoured by the Irish are fluffy, and the sweet white interior swells and cracks the skin, the starchy bit of the spud peeping through invitingly. There would be slabs of butter on the table, little dishes of salt, raw eggs and glasses for the drinks. The youngsters would make mountains of peeled potatoes on their plates and top them with at least two ounces of butter, going back for more later if the spuds were still too dry. Next they put little piles of salt crystals on the side of their plates to dip into (it was bad manners to sprinkle salt all around the place). They could also have cracked an egg or two on to the spuds and mixed them through. Not as bad as it sounds for the heat of the potatoes cooks the eggs, yielding a pile of edible gold. There were jugs of buttermilk on the table and fresh milk thinned down with water to wash everything down. What more could anyone want?

If you were at the Wylies, the meal might be a bit fancier. Still potatoes, but maybe there would be chopped chives on the side and some of their cabbage fried in bacon fat. Nanny Wylie had had some experience of working in the service of big Anglo-Irish households, so the tea would be in a china cup on a saucer. Actually, that is the only way to serve and enjoy tea.

Another heavenly existence. Who could argue with a very large sugar-topped bun for lunch every day, and constant bread and jam and tea on Sundays, and as many potatoes as you wanted for dinner? Then eight of the gang of cousins and friends went off and joined the RAF, one of their school masters joining them in 1939. Two didn't come back.

Later on, my dad also joined the RAF and ended up in Burma serving in the Burma campaign from 1942 to 1945. From then on he began appearing in family photographs on outings with my mother and his sisters in his very smart uniform.

The only thing he ever complained about was being stuck on a troop ship for three months on the way to India. They were fed bully beef and baked beans every day. The home-made butter he was used to was replaced with standard issue Ministry of Defence margarine. During my time at home baked beans never appeared on the grocery list, and at ninety-four my father is still avoiding them. Several thousand servicemen eating baked beans every day for three months in an enclosed space does not bear thinking about.

Having grown up as next-door neighbours, a relationship developed between my parents, and in due course they went to Belfast to buy an engagement ring. When my parents got married in 1953 there was still rationing. How do you throw a wedding party when the dried fruit and butter required for the wedding cake is rationed? Two ounces of butter (50g) per week per individual at the beginning of 1953 and limited dried fruit was not going to help with the making of a wedding cake.

Aunt Sarah, who had been the head cook for the Duke of Manchester at Tandragee Castle, was outraged at the

McKay family meeting. Squeezed into a room that barely measured eight by ten were Aunt Sarah; her sister, my Nanny Wylie; Aunt Maud; Aunt Lila; my mother; and my mother's sister, Evelyn. Aunt Sarah declared, 'There is no such thing as a wedding cake without dried fruit and brandy.' They all looked towards the fireside press, and thought of the quarter bottle of brandy that belonged to my Great-Uncle Frank, who was unmarried and still lived at home, and wondered would he miss a measure or two.

Silence. There was a kitchen press full of strawberry, raspberry, rhubarb, damson and currant jams. There were tons of potatoes in the barn as well as boxes of apples. In the spring, in time for the scheduled wedding date, there would be dozens of eggs, roast chicken for sandwiches no problem, and sugar, plenty in rations. They made their own butter and could provide gallons of cream, so all in all, it was a good start.

'What about a Madeira cake, Sarah?' asked Aunt Lila. 'We don't need one of those big house fancy fruit cakes made to feed an army.'

'Don't be silly. Who ever heard of a Madeira cake for a wedding?'

They all looked at Aunt Sarah, who was used to ordering around a kitchen full of staff and, until the war, had never had to consider where food came from or how much it cost.

Evelyn joined the fray. 'Mary Williamson went down to Monaghan to get the fruit for her cake.'

'What do you mean? Sure who's going to go to Monaghan?

A family picnic. Left to right: Nanny Wylie, Josie, Aunt Lynn, Aunt Ivy, my mother and father. Interesting picnic: no soda bread or tea, sliced-white-bread sandwiches, something in a glass.

There's no bus anyway. You'd have to go to Portadown to catch the train,' said Aunt Sarah.

'We'll go on our bikes,' said my mother.

'Surely not – it's too far,' said Aunt Lila.

'Well, I don't mean Monaghan town. Emyvale is closer and it's stuffed with everything we need. Aren't people going over the border all the time to get things? We could cycle there in about an hour.'

And so they did.

Aunty Bessie's Wedding and Christmas Cake

This recipe is very much of its time and has one pound of currants in it. Currants have fallen off the baking agenda sixty years later and no wonder – if something could be said to taste like the colour black, currants would be the thing. To be kind to currants, I could describe the flavour as being a little bit like liquorice, but this is a stretch. Worse, currants can be gritty. Children view them with suspicion. They may be a hangover from rationing when dried fruits were limited and when currants were more popular, for reasons not at all clear to me. Either way, in my opinion, the best use for currants is as bird food. My dad buys a packet every week for the blackbird that taps on his back door every morning in anticipation of its breakfast. If you try this recipe, you can substitute the currants for something of your own choice, unless you like the taste of black.

Looking at this recipe from the family cookbook now, what really jumps out is the inclusion of ground coriander seeds – in fact, the spices verge on the savoury. Like Black Magic chocolates, the sweetness is in the background.

1lb (400g) currants
½lb (200g) sultanas
¼lb (100g) raisins
½lb (200g) butter
½lb (200g) dark Muscovado sugar
4–5 eggs
½lb (200g) sieved plain flour

1 tsp ground ginger
½ tsp ground allspice
½ tsp ground cinnamon
½ tsp ground cloves
½ tsp ground coriander seeds
¼lb (100g) candied peel
¼lb (100g) glacé cherries
2oz (50g) ground almonds
½ gill (70ml) brandy, whiskey or rum

On the day before baking, wash and dry the dried fruit. The next day, preheat the oven to 150°C, and line a deep 8 inch (20cm) cake tin with a double layer of greaseproof paper. Wrap a double layer of brown paper around the outside of the tin and secure it with string. This is to prevent the outside of the cake becoming dried out before the inside is cooked.

Mix the flour and spices in a bowl. Add one dessert spoon of the mixture to the dried fruit to prevent it from sinking in the cake mix.

Cream together the butter and sugar in a separate bowl, and gradually beat in the eggs, alternating each addition of egg with a spoonful of the flour and spices. Mix in the dried fruit, candied peel, cherries and almonds, and fold in whatever remains of the flour and spices, and pour the mixture into the prepared tin. Bake for three hours.

When the cake is cooked baste it with your preferred spirit. When it has completely cooled, wrap the cake in greaseproof paper and store in an airtight tin (a plastic container will cause the cake to sweat and lead to mould).

3

The Homeplace Kitchens

Before I started school I spent a lot of time at my Nanny Wylie's and at Aunt Lynn's. Lynn was my mother's sister and when she'd married Uncle Joe, she had moved into his Drumreagh (also called Derryvale) homeplace, a three-room thatched cottage on a steep rise above the River Torrent near Coalisland in County Tyrone. The house was exactly a mile out of Coalisland, and about twenty-five minutes from our home in Portadown, so it was easy for my dad to drop me off. Aunt Lynn and Uncle Joe had no children of their own, so I was always welcome, as were my siblings in later years. We enjoyed their lifestyle and they enjoyed our company.

I remember being with my aunt and with my nanny more than I remember being in our prefab in Portadown, so I must have spent a substantial amount of time with them both. To me it was heaven. The arrival of my younger sister when I was three and then my younger brother when I was five limited my freedom. There were nappies and there was a lot of crying – enough for my mother to be doing without having to entertain me as well. Besides, I would always have preferred to be up a tree in Aunt Lynn's orchard or watching my Nanny

Wylie make soda bread on her kitchen table than at home. My grandmother's and aunt's houses provided my parallel homelife. Unbeknownst to me at the time, I was witnessing a cultural transition – a proud and significant rural lifestyle fading into consumerism. I am glad of these early experiences in my rural homeplaces and I carry them with me always. They were a gift of life and sharing and protection and respect, and the best food in the world.

Joe and Lynn's homeplace in Derryvale was up a very long lane on top of a gravelly hill surrounded by a planting of beech trees. To the left of their cottage, just behind the haybarn, the hill plunged down to a former mill stream. A careless step followed by a fall could have been enough to start you rolling right down through the tree-lined gorge and into the river. No one suffered this fate – we were very careful. There were occasional scary slips, which made us shriek, followed by shouts from the house to be careful and to 'stay away from there'.

The bottom of this drop became a sort of car graveyard for all Uncle Joe's old vehicles. Once a car had reached the end of its life and could no longer be patched up, he simply parked the old banger at the top, took off the handbrake, hopped out and gave it a shove. It would gather speed and roll into the gorge. The last time I looked there were at least three car skeletons. It's not as bad as it sounds now, for the run-off and cyclical composting and regrowth of the planting erodes, melts and then finally consumes old Fords and Morris Minors. Bogs throughout Ireland were used for similar purposes because the acidic environment can break down components. Not plastics, though, which is why the dump is the only place for modern materials.

The Ford, long before it was slid down into the car graveyard, and Aunt Lynn on her bike. She never had a driving licence and this was her preferred mode of transport.

My aunt and uncle's nearest neighbours and best friends lived across the river valley gorge. We could see their farmyard and hear them clanging galvanised buckets across their cement yard or running the tractor. They were half a mile away as the crow flies but the only way to reach them was by road. We had risked the rusty old footbridge at the bottom of the gorge for a number of years but more and more bits fell off it until a wise farmer finally tied off both ends with barbed wire.

Often Uncle Joe would be across at the neighbours, helping them out or leaning on the gate and discussing the weekend racing bets. Before my aunt put the spuds on for dinner she would stride across the back field to the highest point, cup her hands around her mouth, and start shouting, 'Joe! Joe!' Then she'd wait for a response. Or she would stick one finger at either side of her mouth and produce a piercing whistle that could have been heard up the valley in Newmills or down towards Coalisland in the other direction. Usually Kenny, the son of the family, would respond with a 'Yoohoo' to let her know she'd been heard. Then my aunt would roar, 'TELL JOE HIS DINNER IS READY.'

The house at Derryvale had been built at a time when public works only put in water pumps for clusters of houses, so they did not get piped water until the seventies. When my uncle was growing up there, living with his parents, three siblings, livestock and no car, how did they get their drinking water? Did they have a horse and cart? Were the children sent off every day with a couple of buckets to walk the quarter of a mile back and forth to the nearest pump to stock up on water for the day? I can only tell you with certainty what happened in 1963. My aunt began: 'Joe, will you go and get some water soon.'

'Aye, all right, in a minute or two.'

'Joe, when are you going?'

'In a minute or two.'

Then he would light a cigarette and sit in front of the big black range that roared like a bull when turf was added to the fire box to boil the spuds, or silently glowed when the cooking was over, all day, every day, summer and winter. He wore navy dungarees that seemed as permanent as the range – I barely remember him in anything else on both the coldest days and the hottest days. If it was snowing he would put a tweed jacket on, perhaps a flat cap to go out to the 'beasts'.

'Joe, will you go and get water!'

'I'm going now.' He opened the front door of the range and fired in the cigarette butt.

To go for the water, my uncle put two milk churns in the boot of the car, drove down the lane and took a sharp left at the junction of the three roads there – one to Coalisland, one to Brackaville and one leading to Newmills. Facing this junction were two fields belonging to my aunt and uncle's farm. Above the fields was a small cluster of cottages, one of which supplied milk to the local houses. Another daily chore, as well as fetching the water, involved walking there, having a good old catch-up with the neighbours, collecting the milk and then walking back. Opposite the lane to these cottages on the other side of the road was the water pump that served my aunt and uncle's farm and the cottages. It was a quarter of a mile away.

When he reached the iron water pump, Joe would have to draw the water into the milk churns by vigorously raising and lowering the handle mechanism that pumped the water up from the supply. Next he would have to lift the two heavy churns into the car boot and then out again back at the house.

One time, when my brother and sister had got over being babies, and my mother was not well, Aunt Lynn found herself with three youngsters to look after. We ran out of water when my uncle was at work. My aunt organised us children with a bucket each and two for her and off we went to the pump. She jollied us along, of course, and we stopped for many rests and laughs – quite a bit of time was spent playing 'pumping' and getting soaked – and probably got back with about half the water we started with, but we had tea till Joe got back from work and were able to boil the spuds.

We used to wash our faces and hands in a basin of water drawn from a wooden barrel positioned at the side of the cottage to catch rainwater from the down spout. It was good for washing hair – made it soft and shiny. Too bad about it being cold. Laundry? I can't remember where the water came from. Sometimes I helped turn the mangle, as it was entertaining for me, but the advantage of being a small inquisitive child is that you are more in the way than helpful.

There was a little lean-to that had been added as an afterthought to the cottage that connected the backyard to the house. It was a scullery – a functional room for food preparation – and it also acted as a washroom, with the mangle and washtub sitting just outside the door. There were always two white enamel buckets of drinking water on the floor of this room. The water always stayed cool and nothing ever seemed to drop into the buckets to spoil it. The roof was low and made of corrugated iron. Its four-pane window (unopenable) was decorated with a gingham curtain and was quite low down so you could only see through it when you sat at the scullery table. None of this mattered because, unless it was night or there was driving snow or rain, the back door was always open. Like in our prefab kitchen, there was a Belfast sink, only without running water, and a wooden drainer. There was another gingham curtain drawn across the space under the sink and the bench. Here, the scrubbing brush lived with cleaning liquids like ammonia and stove black, and the household toiletries (one bar of Lifebuoy soap, a tin of toothpaste and my uncle's Brylcreem). The smell of a soap bar of Sunlight, the size of a brick, that my aunt used for handwashing clothes, seemed always to permeate the room.

Hens and neighbours and the cat and dog could wander in. The hens would be shooed away, the cat offered heart-stopping full-cream milk, and the neighbours a cup of strong tea that looked like yacht varnish. Mostly the dog did not bother coming in, except at our teatime, and he slept outside in the barn.

Just like at my own house there were always buns – here they were kept in a tin in the sideboard in the main living room. The range was here too, on which a four-pint kettle steamed gently like a sleeping volcano, its water always ready to make tea.

Although most of the food preparation took place in the scullery, we always had to keep an eye on the range

Uncle Joe at the house at Derryvale.

because it had to be stoked for any cooking or baking. One of my jobs was to watch the needle on the oven door thermostat and alert my aunt when it got to the right place. All this extra heat would bring the perpetually boiling kettle to a crescendo. If the boiling got too violent then someone would move the kettle off the direct heat and sit it beside the tin teapot at the back of the range.

Tea in this pot brewed for several hours. If someone wanted a quick cuppa and it was low in liquid then they topped it up with water from the kettle. There is good value in making tea this way for tea leaves are amazingly long lasting.

An older system still remained in many rural households at this time, where the centre of operations in the house was an enormous fireplace. All of these iconic whitewashed thatched cottages consisted of three rooms, the middle being the living area. Usually there was a porch for the main entrance, a bedroom to the left and living room to the right and centre. On the dividing wall between the bedroom and living area would have been the fireplace over which the family cooked in black crocks. The very last time I was in such a house was 2002 in Leitrim near Hilltown in County Down. The two elderly sisters I was visiting had lived there all their lives, and must have made a decision not to change anything, for there were many opportunities over the years to modernise with government grants. These women had conceded only to having a two-ring cylinder gas stove that sat on an old TV table covered with plastic. The fire in their traditional large open fireplace never went out and after I had sat beside it for a few minutes, I never wanted to move again. I felt transported back to the familiar cosiness of my childhood.

Killyman, a couple of miles away, was my maternal grandmother's home. I was often taken there in a child's seat on the back of my Aunt Lynn's bike from Drumreagh. Although Nanny Wylie was the oldest member of the family, she had the most modern kitchen of all, for in the early fifties she had been rehoused in a small brand-new redbrick rural housing development, a few miles from their previous home in Cohannon. It still had no fridge, for why should it? Lucy's shop was a short walk away – Lucy stocked nearly everything, then her husband Wullie delivered your order. The butcher, fishmonger and milkman came round in their vans, and Granda Wylie grew vegetables (though on a smaller scale than he had done on the Bovean Road).

In this very modern 1950s house, the kitchen was located at the front. I liked this arrangement – I still do today and have arranged my current house that way. Spending so much time there, as many women did in those days, a kitchen at the front meant you could see all the goings-on in the street. You could anticipate the arrival of visitors and delivery men, and the living room was private with a view to the garden.

Being farmed out to my maternal grandmother a lot as a child, I became her helper in the kitchen. At four years old I was tall enough, just, to keep watch for the groceries from Lucy's shop. I would stand with my fingertips on the windowsill, which was level with my watching eyes. Snuff the dog always heard the sound of the delivery van before anyone else, and would leap up from his spot by the fire in the sitting room and bark like fury. At that point I would climb up on a chair to see if I could get a better view. Then the van would pull up and Wullie, who wore the same type of blue dungarees as Uncle Joe, would bring in the box of goods.

'Are you keeping well, Mrs Wylie?'

'Yes thank you, Wullie. How is Lucy?'

'Oh, keeping well, nothing to complain about. See you

next week.' And off he went to the next house.

It was my job to put away the groceries. As my grandmother unpacked the items, I got down off the chair to open the larder door – the larder was shallow but covered an entire wall, and consisted of an upper half and a lower half: the groceries went in the bottom half, the best china was in the top. When the door opened, there was a waft of cheese, bacon, butter, sugar, bread. I often wandered into the kitchen to open the larder door a crack just to experience the aroma. My grandmother kept all the dry goods in tins. Tins are a good system: airtight and damp-proof, they stack well and last for decades. Each bore a striking image advertising its contents: the Bisto tin was adorned with a boy who had a pointy nose and wore a strange hat, the illustration set off by a brown background the same colour as the gravy. He looked over two primary-school-age children, happy to be having gravy poured over their spuds. But Bisto to me was an inferior choice, for the best way to serve potatoes was with a big chunk of butter melting down the side like a lava flow, the steam rising like an eruption from Mount Kilimanjaro.

The salt tin bore a blue illustration of a boy about to pour salt on a blackbird, frozen to the spot, poor wee thing. Why did it not take off? Clearly something bad was about to happen, and I did not like this for I knew boys in short trousers were often wicked towards animals, especially birds. They always seemed to want to shoot them with pellet guns or take their eggs. When I asked my grandmother why the boy was pouring salt on the blackbird, she said that it was because a bird with salt on its tail couldn't fly. So the boy was using the salt as a means to capture the poor wee thing. The point of the ad being, I suppose, that the salt was fast flowing enough to catch a bird.

My grandmother had a superb porcelain cheese bell, about nine inches in diameter, its ornately decorated lid edged with gold. The handle was a swirl of rose branch, also highlighted with gold. She got it in an auction – it had come from one of the big houses in the area, most of which had gone into decline. The lid was heavy and big for a child to lift when the new block of cheese needed to go in, but as a careful child I was trusted with the job. Next I would check the butter dish – a porcelain box with a resting cow as the handle.

I put the cans – peas and peaches – on a narrow shelf at the back of the larder. I was not allowed to empty the flour into the flour bin for both the bag and the bin were nearly as big as me. The cloth bag held half a stone (3kg) of flour, enough for soda bread for the week. I might be allowed to replenish the sugar bowl from the bag if it was well down and there were no sticky bits in it. The sugar bowl was also grand, cut glass with three legs. After that it was eggs, porridge, tea and some household stuff like Brillo pads or washing powder. My grandmother got bacon and ham on her daily walk and the bread was home baked.

I was ready for a farl of soda bread, which was being mixed as I helped with the unpacking. The kitchen table was the place of all these activities – a central control hub from which all angles of the household could be observed and conversations conducted, a gathering-together of all good things in the kitchen. Whoever thought of work benches which put your back to the action? As I put away the last tins and took the baking soda out of the larder, my grandmother assembled everything: buttermilk from the doorstep, a mixing bowl, flour and salt. She put a griddle sprinkled with flour on the stove to heat up and the magic began. Nanny Wylie measured out the ingredients by instinct in handfuls. I never saw her use scales for anything. She was as quick as a magician putting the mix together, and possibly could have made the bread with her eyes closed. I was content enough to sit at the table and watch and wait. In went the flour, swiftly followed by baking soda and salt, then enough buttermilk to hold it all together in a dough that was manageable enough to be turned out on the floured table. She lightly kneaded it then formed it into two circles, each of which she cut into quarters and plopped on to the hot griddle. After a couple of minutes, the farls were flipped over and finished cooking on the other side. The cooked bread was laid out on a cooling tray and covered with a tea towel.

'Nanny Wylie, how can you make the bread without using scales?'

'What would I need scales for?'

'Well, Mummy always uses scales when she is baking.'

'I just know,' she would say to me, for I asked many times. 'Look. Watch.'

And I did, dozens of times, but I could never figure out entirely what magic was going on, or reproduce the quality of the bread when I tried to many years later.

There is something in bakery soda bread that gives me indigestion but her farls were nice and thin, very difficult to reproduce as the dough had to be strong enough to handle, but not so strong that it became dense. It's delicious for one day and any bread left over the next day – there was rarely any – was fried on the pan.

She washed up the baking things, wiped the oilcloth-covered kitchen table and asked me to set it with cups, saucers and plates as she made the tea. We would then sit down together for a cuppa and I would get my reward. A piece of soda bread, still warm enough to melt the butter, and then the treat: sugar sprinkled on top.

Nanny Wylie's Griddle Soda Farls

4oz (100g) plain flour, plus extra for dusting
¼ level tsp baking soda (bicarbonate of soda)
¼ tsp salt
Around 200ml buttermilk

You will need a traditional griddle pan for this or, if you don't have one, a good heavy frying pan of at least 12 inches (30cm) in diameter, and a rolling pin.

Put the pan over a medium heat. To test if the pan is at the correct temperature, sprinkle some flour on it. The flour should go brown in about three minutes.

Sieve the dry ingredients into a mixing bowl, then pour enough buttermilk in to bring the mixture together into an elastic dough. It should be springy and stretchy. Too much liquid and it will be sticky; too little and it will be tough. Concentrate on the consistency.

Dust your hands, the rolling pin and your worktop with some flour, and tip the soda bread dough out on to the worktop.

Shape the dough into a ball and then knead it until smooth. Do not turn it over and do not get carried away – overworking is a killer for this bread: it will make it tough and you will be disappointed. Now turn it over and keeping the dough round roll it out evenly to the thickness of about half an inch. Cut into quarters (these are your farls) and place them on the heated pan.

Now you have to watch – there is no formulaic description of exactly how this will go. Use your nose and eyes. The farls will start to puff up and, after about three minutes or so, you will smell warm cooked flour. Using a palette knife, flip a farl over – it should be golden brown. If not, leave it and the others for another couple of minutes before turning them all over. After another three minutes, do a 'spring' test: when pushed down lightly, the farl should spring up. If any of the surfaces look anaemic, give them another minute each. If the flour starts to smell bitter, get the bread off the griddle as quickly as you can.

Place it on a cooling tray and cover it with a clean tea towel.

The secrets to this recipe are dough consistency and temperature control of the griddle. Definitely worth practising.

Serve warm with plenty of butter and home-made jam, washed down with strong leaf tea. Very good with boiled eggs or fried eggs and bacon. People's new favourite is a filled soda, the Northern Irish burger, I suppose: just pop your fry items between a sliced farl.

4

3lb Butter and a Packet of Lard

A page from one of my mother's grocery books.

'Oh Mummy, can we have Dairylea cheese as well? Janet says you can spread it on a slice of bread and toast it. She says it's *really* delicious and I want to try it,' I pleaded as we walked to the shops.

'Okay, we'll see, we'll see,' said my mother, going back to her grocery book.

This was a risky request but one worth trying (I might be given a dispensation) because the decision about what groceries to buy was made before my mother left the house for her weekly shop. She would sit down at the kitchen table, after breakfast and after checking the larder shelves, and make a list in her grocery book of what she needed. I still have these books and I can spot when there were birthdays or visitors on the horizon because the list then had exotic items on it, like 'tin of fruit salad'. I found a reference to 'greengage jelly'. I wonder what this was for, possibly a treat for afters for Sunday lunch, the only day of the week when we would have had more than one course.

Such exotic items did not appear on the table on school days. Friday was fish, always. During the rest of the week, for our evening meals, we'd have liver, sausages, stew, mince and bacon. If my mother got a new cookery book, or was inspired by something in one of her magazines, we might come home to stuffed beef olives, or meatloaf, or – the best one ever – Hungarian goulash. At 3 p.m. each day she would start peeling potatoes and vegetables, and preparing whatever she had decided on for the evening meal that day. My dad parked his yellow post office van in the post office yard each day at 4 p.m. and was home by 4.30 with an empty lunch box and empty stomach, having worked outside all day, whatever the weather. As a child I remember seeing half a loaf of cheese sandwiches going into his lunchbox one morning.

We walked to the shops, always. In fact, we walked everywhere, unless our destination was more than five miles away, in which case we'd get a bus or travel by bike, and we enjoyed it. My mother couldn't drive, so even when Dad's car was parked outside the house we walked. In 1960s Ireland, during shop opening hours, the streets were full of women, head-scarfed and with shopping baskets. They would meet their friends out on the same errands, and catch up with the gossip – back then, news travelled just as fast by word of mouth as it does today via Facebook.

There was daily shopping as well; fridges, like cars, were a rarity, so if you wanted a quarter-pound of sliced cooked ham you went and got it. In spite of our fridge at home, it took many years until my mother bought perishable goods in advance of the day they were needed. Even if a woman in the 1960s had access to a car, it was not helpful for grocery shopping as the weekly order of goods was always delivered, and it was unimaginable that anyone would put food in the back of the car. Anything could go wrong: the tea packet could burst, the eggs were in an open tray and could break, and flour bags were cloth and gave off pleasing little cloudbursts of white powder every time they moved. No, definitely no groceries in the family car that was polished weekly to within an inch of its life inside and out.

We shopped at McQuillan's in Edgarstown, Portadown, our nearest grocery shop during the years that I was at preschool and in Primary 1. It was about ten minutes' walk from our house. It had a butcher's shop on one side and a draper's on the other. Across the road was a bakery, which we never entered because we baked everything ourselves. Next to that was an American-style diner – but we never ate out. Occasionally we had home-made chips. The aroma of the chips from the diner was intriguing to me, though. It wasn't until many years later when friends shared their chips with me that I got to try them.

Entering McQuillan's we were met by a square block of Cheddar cheese, nearly as big as my baby brother, sitting on the marble slab on the wooden counter. I was just big enough at five to see over the top and look longingly at the shop assistant dealing with our order, for my mother, like everyone else who bought cheese in the shop, was given a sliver for approval before purchase, especially if it was a new block being opened, cheese being a variable thing. I might not be included in this tasting event as children were generally ignored, but I could look hopeful just in case.

Typically, a block of cheese weighed fourteen pounds (slightly over six kilos). Once the block was all sold the shop assistant would have to go into the store, then into the walk-in refrigerator, and lift a new block of cheese to bring out to the counter. He or she may have encountered any variety of shop workers or delivery men on this journey and they would have all exchanged greetings and jokes, for there was no hurry except for the tea or lunch break, or at home time. All the while, whoever was waiting on their order of cheese would have stood patiently – there were almost always plenty of neighbours and friends with whom to pass the time. Having tasted and approved the cheese, my mother would ask Mr Cyril to cut 8oz (200g) for her. He split the larger block into four with a cheese wire – one end of which had what looked like a cricket stump for him to grip, the other nailed to the wooded counter. I studied his actions as he lifted the slice of cheese with a piece of greaseproof paper and carefully placed it on the scales adjacent to the marble block – he always cut exactly the right amount. The scales were like those on top of the Royal Courts of Justice. Cyril nodded at my mother who nodded back. He knew I was waiting patiently for my taste of cheese but he always finished my mother's order before I got my reward. It only took him a matter of seconds to tear off a piece of brown paper from the roll in the holder, wrap the cheese and secure the package with string. Then, he put it into the cardboard carton already containing the other items on my mother's grocery list. With a grand gesture of the cheese wire he slowly cut a tiny sliver of cheese and reached over the counter to hand it to me. I just about managed to say thanks before popping it into my mouth. 'Right, Mrs Farrell,' said Mr Cyril, 'what's next on your list?'

Grocery shops then were small affairs, with more or less everything behind a sturdy wooden counter that held deep secret shelves on the inside. Behind each counter stood the staff, mostly men and always wearing a white coat of heavyweight cotton that required scrubbing, bleaching, starching and ironing by a wife or mother to be pristine enough for work. Behind the staff, the walls were lined with box shelves from floor to ceiling, filled with products such as tinned fruits and meats, jams for those who didn't make their own, Bisto, mustard, tinned soup and cocoa. Usually, tea, flour and sugar were weighed out to order. The floor, made of bare boards, was scrubbed to within an inch of its life at the end of every day.

Only after consultation with the shopping list, the shop assistant and any neighbours close by would my mother make a purchase. She ticked off each item with the seriousness of a customs officer who knows that every crumb has a value. No one was throwing money about on a whim. However, my mother was adventurous about food and baking, always ready to try the new products displayed temptingly on the counters. I remember when Angel Delight, a sort of instant mousse, arrived in the shop and she went for it. It was okay but really we preferred a home-made bun for supper.

Along the ceiling, suspended on S-shaped hooks, sharp at both ends, hung joints of bacon. My mother always ordered a pound of back and breakfast (this is a cut that includes the loin and streaky all on one piece, not split into two different cuts as we often see nowadays). The shop assistant unhooked the appropriate joint and sliced the bacon there and then. As the manually operated circular blade cut through the cured meat, it made a 'sssss' noise. The bacon slicer was designed to move the joint back and forth against the spinning blade and the shop assistant caught the individual slices, put them on some greaseproof paper, then weighed the pile. When these rashers went on the pan, there was no seepage, nor was there the milky froth we get nowadays, for bacon was dry cured then, the rind sparkling like rhinestones from the little flecks of salt, and it always crisped up into a honey-coloured band of flavour. My mother never bought streaky bacon – 'not substantial enough'.

Sometimes, when a customer wanted a particular brand of peaches from the top shelf, the shop assistant needed a ladder. If he or she wanted to show off, they would get a window pole, hold it in one hand, knock the can off the shelf with the hook at the end of the pole and catch the can with the other. This usually got a cheer. I never remember anyone dropping anything or falling off a ladder from over-reaching although I do remember watching in silence with everyone else, waiting just in case – it was crowded behind the shop counter, with many assistants scurrying back and forth, and the ladder was frequently nudged.

A couple of years later when we moved from our prefab, which was to be pulled down for redevelopment, to a brick-built house on the Garvaghy Road beside Portadown Park, the trip to our new grocer became scary. It should have been fun because it began with a cut across the town park where Mary Peters, the Olympic gold medal winner, trained as a young woman. We also had football pitches, a cycle dome, a duck pond, bowls, tennis courts and a wonderful children's playground with a tarmacadam surface. Tragically one of our young friends died there when he flew off the swing and hit the ground, probably as hard as someone in a traffic accident. After that I was highly suspicious of the playground and liked to hurry past. The rest of the walk to the new grocer, Emerson's, was pleasant enough and I could run around on the grass or climb a tree until my mother caught up. At the exit from the park I started to get uneasy again, for next we had to run the gauntlet under the railway bridge. To be caught underneath when the Dublin steam train passed over, screeching its parting whistle as it left the station with coal smoke descending around us, felt like being in the middle of an erupting volcano. The first time it happened I froze. If I was with my mother she would take my hand and we would run. If I ever went into the town on my own, I walked the extra half-mile round the streets to avoid the bridge entirely.

Before we children arrived, the grocery book shows that my parents used about a pound and a half of butter each week. When all three children had arrived, the five of us used to walk to Emerson's in Carlton Street, which had become more advanced by the mid-sixties, and I'd be sent to the long refrigerated display fridge at the back of the shop to lift three pounds of butter. We still had a list but by then we collected the goods from the shelves ourselves. We then went to a checkout where the assistant keyed each item into the till and packed everything into a cardboard box. I liked this new system that allowed me to get up close to the food and explore each aisle until my parents called me.

At the same time that Emerson's in Portadown became automated, my future husband Richard was working his first job, forty miles away in Rostrevor, at his local grocery store. The worst thing he had to do was nail tin-can lids over holes in the wooden floor to stop the rats getting in. The best thing? Well, he was responsible for deliveries on one of those bikes that had a holder on the front big enough to take a box of groceries. A hundred years earlier, he might have slept under the counter in one of the deep shelves.

He got out quite a lot and earned his frys by cycling uphill for miles to dignified and kind elderly ladies, remnants of the British Empire in crumbling but grand houses. In January they waited for the delivery of marmalade oranges to come in so that they could make a batch of marmalade for the year. In midsummer it was soft fruits for jam. Outside of that he made the weekly trek with their orders that, like ours at home, had been carefully composed then checked off in the grocery shop. I would not be surprised if their orders were similar to ours. We didn't have lots of choice in the fifties and sixties. When one of these wonderful old characters opened the kitchen door where the groceries were dropped off at the appointed time, there was a waft of warm air from a range carrying a hint of lavender and boiled cabbage and ham, with overtones of dog, or cat, or tobacco. There was always a glass of home-made lemonade for Richard and half a crown tip at Christmas. He did all right.

No one bought milk in the shops as the milkman left however many pint bottles you needed on the doorstep every morning before 7 a.m. We got three pints; our neighbours with ten children took eight. All we had to do was wash the empty bottles the night before and place them on the doorstep. As if by magic, in the morning there would be three full bottles in their place, fresher than we ever experience nowadays, and creamier. You could either shake the bottle to disperse the settled layer of cream before pouring or, like me, you could siphon off the cream for your porridge before anyone else used it. Along with the milk crates, he also carried a crate of bottles of orange drink on the float. Occasionally in the summer, my mother would leave a note for the milkman: 'Please leave 1 pint of Sukie orange.' A rare treat for us.

Milk then was not homogenised – homogenisation is the process by which the fat content of the milk is integrated throughout the white liquid – and without a fridge it had a very short life. That was okay, for it if went off we used it as a buttermilk substitute. Unless you are lucky enough to live near a dairy, you will never see milk as it used to be. This is sad because a pint of milk could have had about four ounces of cream on top, depending on the herd of cows. A typical plastic container of milk is blended from many different dairy herds and has no particular characteristics. Until my early twenties I could identify the dairy from which milk had come by its taste and from the amount of cream on top. I tried always to get milk from a dairy I liked. Draynes was my favourite – they make ice cream now as well as other dairy produce from their own herd of cows, and are proud of the creaminess of their milk.

The milkman collected payment on a Friday evening, still wearing his white coat and peaked dairy hat. He had a leather satchel containing the payments and change and a foolscap-sized ledger with the record of sales. I remember standing on the doorstep on a Friday evening, watching the proceedings as usual. I was particularly interested when he raised his leather satchel to eye level and tipped it back so that he could find the change he needed. He could do this without any of the money falling out – the flap on the bag acted as a sort of tray.

In my husband's part of the world, the milkman came in for a cup of tea on Friday evening when he called in to be paid. It could be late for he collected a few bevvies on the way round the streets. My mother-in-law always worried about him being inebriated in charge of a milk van so she made him a fry and he and my father-in-law talked football for an hour or so. Sometimes he would fall asleep in front of the coal-fired Stanley range, and at bedtime they would shake him and send him on his way. They were his last stop, so this isn't quite as bad as it sounds. He could walk back to where he started from.

The cows that produced the milk were in the fields around their house, so close you could hear them munching the grass. I live in that house now but if I want a pint of milk I have to walk or drive for my plastic carton or bottle.

Two pounds of sugar and quarter of a pound of tea are almost always at the top of each list in my mother's grocery book. Most of the sugar went into the tea – there may have been two sugars for each cup, or more. There was always a sugar bowl on the table and it was refilled regularly. If my friends came round – usually three or four from the neighbouring houses; we were always a troop – I offered them tea. We drank tea from when we were no age but we did not make it until we were seven or so – then it was safe to be in charge of boiling water among other things. The age of visiting children ranged from about three years old to seven, for the bigger ones included the wee ones in games and outings. I remember some of the kids just about being able to hold their cup. There was extra milk in it to stop them getting scalded. Then, of course, there was the sugar.

'How many spoonfuls do you take?' asked Maureen, with her eyebrows raised and her scratched legs swinging back and forward under the table, after my mother had gone to chat to Maureen's mother across the fence. We all looked at each other. My preference was to take none but I knew this was going to be a competition, so I decided to wait to find out what the others were going to say. I definitely didn't want to go too high for I didn't like sugar in my tea – but it was just something everybody did. In fact, it was pretty much compulsory. Maureen was in charge of toddler Billy, who was her brother. She began spooning sugar into his cup.

'Say when, Billy,' she said in a posh voice, as if we were having tea somewhere grand. Billy kept nodding his head, his little fat fingers grasping the edge of the table.

'Stop it, Maureen!' said her sister Jane. 'You know he's only allowed five spoonfuls.'

Billy nodded, then stood on the chair, lifted the cup and drained the lot. 'More, more, more …'

'Sit down, Billy,' ordered Maureen. 'Now Susan, how

many sugars do *you* have?'

I was not impressed. I was in my own house and being bossed around, so decided not to play: 'Well, actually, I don't like sugar in my tea.'

'For goodness' sake, whoever heard of anybody not taking sugar in their tea?'

Jane decided to side with me, probably at the risk of getting a thump on the way home. 'Well, some people don't, Maureen,' she said, sipping her meagre three-spoon cup of tea.

'I prefer dipping my Marie biscuit in my tea. Too much sugar will rot your teeth and you'll have to go to the dentist,' I told them.

'See if I care. I take five sugars. So there.'

We slurped our tea and thought about the dentist silently for a while. Billy started to whimper about going home. Maureen swigged the remains of syrupy tea, gathered up her clan and left shouting, 'See ya tomorrow.' They had entirely emptied the crystal-cut sugar bowl except for a few congealed lumps. I washed out the bowl at the sink with a generous dollop of Fairy Liquid and the squeegee, then gave it a good polish with the tea towel until it shone like a crystal chandelier. Next, I stood on a chair to reach the sugar on the top shelf of the larder. I refilled the bowl, then put in a clean spoon, ready for the next session of tooth-rotting tea.

My mother came in the back door with an armful of washing from the line and said, 'Clear the table, Susan – the groceries are here.' Our order had arrived on the back of the delivery lorry that was parked at the end of lane. All our neighbours' orders were also on board. Unless there was rain, the canvas canopy remained tied up on a frame above the flat bed, like a giant tent with its sides rolled up. Mothers and children from the six or so prefab bungalows assembled round the lorry as the driver handed over our boxes. He wore a flat hat, collarless shirt and his trousers were held up with braces.

He had a pencil balanced on the top of his ear. I tried many times as a child and sometimes as an adult to get a pencil to balance in this way for handiness' sake, but my ears must lack whatever is needed to achieve this – maybe they are not big enough. A cigarette drooped from the side of his mouth. It never interfered with his constant joking as he went around the houses or with his barging and cajoling with the boys on the street, who all wanted to climb up on to the lorry and sit there, swinging their legs, as he continued on his round. He stopped frequently to shoo them away, or braked suddenly to jolt them off. If someone fell, they just howled with laughter.

Like all the children on our street, I went to the lorry to help my mother carry the groceries back into the house. We'd unpack the boxes and put each item on the table so that my mother could check them against both the docket and her grocery book. Everything had to tally. She paid our account at a different time – I have no idea why everyone ran accounts, but they did. Perhaps it was, in part, for hygiene reasons – it is bad practice to handle raw foods and money as part of the same transaction. The butchers and bakers took cash payments, but it was always someone separate who handled the money.

I usually helped put the groceries away. There was a tin for the seriously depleted sugar; a bin for our regular delivery of six pounds of flour; and a tea caddy for the loose tea. The cheese went on to a flat ceramic plate with a glass dome on top. Butter packets were stacked at the back of the larder until needed. I enjoyed putting everything away, for I loved the smells of the food items and looked forward to whatever they were going turn into, and there was the anticipation of what anything new or different might mean: visitors or a birthday party or a cookery experiment. Usually, anything new would have been inspired by *Woman's Weekly* or *Woman's Realm*. One week the surprise item was Camp Coffee. I examined the label; a kilted soldier beside a tent being served a cup of coffee by a sheik holding a tray. My mother told me she was going to make a coffee cake at the weekend.

'I'm going to make a drink of coffee. Do you want to try some?' she said to me. I never refused anything and knew too that this would be a good topic of conversation for school the next day.

I nodded yes and watched the procedure. A teaspoonful of a brown syrupy liquid topped up with boiling water and some milk in a china cup, always on a saucer. I wasn't too sure about this concoction but I guessed that few of my friends would have tried coffee. The reality of Camp Coffee is that the main ingredient is sugar, about 70 per cent, then chicory at 25 per cent and coffee at 4 per cent. My sugar-loving friends would like this better than me. I slurped it down anyway and said, 'Very nice, thank you,' to my mother and hoped that the cake would taste better.

Coffee and Walnut Sandwich

Sponge
5oz (125g) butter
5oz (125g) caster sugar
2 medium eggs
1floz (25ml) Camp Coffee
5oz (125g) sieved plain flour
1 level tsp baking powder
2oz (50g) chopped walnuts

Filling
3oz (75g) soft butter
3oz (75g) icing sugar
1 tbsp Camp Coffee
1oz (25g) chopped walnuts

Preheat the oven to 200°C.

Cream the butter and sugar until the mixture is pale in colour. Beat in the eggs and Camp Coffee. Don't worry if the mixture looks quite loose. Sieve the flour and baking powder into the mixture and fold in. Then add the walnuts.

Divide the mixture between two cake tins and bake for about 25 minutes, until the sponge springs to the touch. Turn out on to a cooling rack.

To make the filling, cream the butter and icing sugar together until the mixture is smooth and pale. Add the coffee essence and walnuts. When the sponge is cool, sandwich the two halves together with the coffee buttercream.

If you want to push the boat out, use some Camp Coffee to make glacé icing for the top.

5

Cake Sundays

After church and a pot-roast lunch on a Sunday, we often went visiting, especially in the summer when there was no Sunday school. The traffic was all one way: us to the homeplaces, for my dad had a car and we were the part of the family that did the visiting. We most often went to my mother's family as we were the only children on that side. We visited my father's family less because there were many more cousins on his side, and my paternal grandparents were elderly and, having brought up eleven children of their own, probably quite enjoyed a bit of peace and quiet. But we did go round regularly, on shorter visits, and my mother and Granny Farrell were great friends.

Sunday afternoon actually started on Saturday morning, for there were baked goods to be made. A Victoria sponge was compulsory. Depending on who we were visiting we might also make lemon meringue pie, gingerbread, angel cakes or all of these things. At certain times of year there might also be apple or rhubarb tart, and as we got close to Hallowe'en, we'd make apple dumpling, finishing the year with Christmas cake. Saturdays also included cleaning the house in order to leave us free the next day for church, lunch, visiting, walking, tea and maybe some free time after that to read or play cards.

By the age of ten, it was no bother for me to read a recipe and follow the instructions. I loved helping to make the gingerbread, for example. I reached down the flour bin, the sugar bin, Stork margarine, treacle, eggs and little tubs of spices from the larder and put them all on the kitchen table. Our scales were the balancing type – a cream-and-green base with stainless steel trays, not dissimilar to the scales used in the baby clinic to keep track of babies' growth. I tried my doll – she weighed eight ounces. Next I got out the earthenware baking bowl, light brown on the outside and white on the inside, a wooden spoon, a scraper and some spoons. That's all you need, apart from cake tins. My job was to put eight ounces of margarine with two big dollops of treacle into a saucepan and, standing on a chair, stir it on the cooker until the margarine melted. Meanwhile my mother started to prepare the dry ingredients – I could smell the ginger as soon as the lid was off the tub. While my mother mixed in the eggs and then folded in the flour, I greased the inside of a loaf tin using the scraps of margarine on the margarine paper, then sprinkled in a dusting of flour. Once the needle on the oven was at 325, my mother popped the loaf tin into the oven, then started on the bun mix.

My treat was scraping out the baking bowl. Suddenly my brother and sister appeared from nowhere and began sticking their fingers in the bowl.

'Go away, this is mine.'

'No, it's not.'

'Go away, I did the baking.'

'No, you didn't – Mummy did.'

'I did the margarine in the treacle and some of the creaming.'

'See if I care.'

Then they ran off because there were still the dishes to be washed. I had the last laugh, though, because I turned out to be the best cook and made my living at it for a while. And when I was a cook there was somebody else to do the dishes.

One Sunday we went to visit Aunt Lynn who had previously been on a cookery course at the tech. There were rumours of a Swiss roll – only seen before in bakeries. They were considered very difficult to make because of the risk of the egg sponge collapsing or being too difficult to roll, but now Aunt Lynn had been on a course we expected that she would have it all worked out. There was great excitement on the Saturday evening. I asked my mother 'Will there be cream and jam in the filling?'

'Lynn said jam – it's too warm for cream.'

'What sort of jam?'

'Raspberry.'

'The jam she made the other week?'

'Think so.'

It was the end of July: the hay had been cut and all the soft fruit jam made so the visit was likely to involve a walk up some rarely used back lane. The thorn hedging would probably meet in the middle and there was bound to be an overhang of bramble. The adults would simply pull stout sticks out of the hedge and beat down the offending branches. I'd be obliged to wear a dress, so I could look forward to scratched legs.

There were a few routes to Aunt Lynn's. Quite often, before the motorway was built, we used the road that went towards Maghery. It seemed to be heading directly into the lough and then, at the last minute, it turned suddenly to the left. The road was constructed this way so that carts and vehicles could get to the edge of the lough to collect catches of fish.

Kate Duff, known locally as Kate the Fish, walked in her bare feet from here to Dungannon, a distance of ten miles, with a basket of fish on her head in the 1930s, when my parents were children. She was well known to everyone because she stopped off for rests and a drink of water and to deliver fish along the way. I suspect she got a lift now and again on a cart, for if you knew her, and everyone did, you would offer a lift out of neighbourliness. A surviving picture shows her dressed as all women of this generation were, in a black skirt, a wool cardigan over a blouse of some sort, and a black shawl tied round her waist. She wore a leather apron – maybe it was because of her work, for the fish would have had to be cleaned. She probably lived in a dark smoky thatched cottage somewhere in the area because she was known to labour on local farms. I hope she treated herself to a large piece of bacon with her spuds in the evening after covering twenty miles, mostly on foot, or an eight ounce salmon steak, then toasted herself in front of the turf fire, and washed it all down with tea so strong it looked like tar and so sweet it made you sit up straight, or maybe sent you to sleep, for that is what I would have done after walking twenty miles.

For years and years at Maghery, where the road met Lough Neagh, there were nets stretched out to dry across five-foot-high frames, as if to catch birds instead of fish. Occasionally I would see the fishermen and women either hanging the nets or taking them down. At other times they would be checking for damage, retying knots and stitching, frozen in time like an old Jean-François Millet painting. This place seemed like a busy fishing port to me, and Lough Neagh was an ocean, stretching out infinitely.

Even as a child, it was striking to me that we never got out to explore here, as was our wont in the most interesting places. My parents thought nothing of stopping the car if they spotted wild mushrooms in a field. They would simply climb over the gate, shoo away any annoying cows and help themselves. If the farmer or landowner appeared, they would exchange greetings and talk about the benefits of field mushrooms. We were never turned away – our foraging then just seemed a neighbourly sharing and anyway the cows usually trampled the mushrooms into the ground if they were not picked. At other times we might stop to pick damson plums from a hedgerow for jam. As I drive about in the autumn, if I catch sight of what might be ripe damsons, I pull in to have a look. Damson jam is my favourite, and wild damsons are a rare bounty these days, and one for which it's worth holding up traffic on a narrow road. The reward is the richest-tasting jam of all. In the winter I can cosy up in front of the fire with hot buttered soda bread and damson jam and laugh at the memory of the queue of cars waiting to pull round me, the drivers wondering what on earth I am doing.

We did not stop on the lough to find out if it was eels or rudd or salmon being caught there. We did not even chat about it when one of us children would say, 'What's those nets for?' The short answer – 'fish' – came in a tone of voice that indicated there would be no more information forthcoming. So none of us said 'What type of fish?' or 'Can we go and look?' We just knew we weren't stopping and that there was no point in asking any more questions.

I always thought it was because we were in a hurry to get visiting but many years later, when I was telling my mother that I was going on a boating trip down the Shannon, it all came out.

'But how will you find your way on the river?'

'There are maps.'

'Yes, but what if there is a storm, what will you do?'

'Pull in somewhere – there's plenty of places to tie the boat up. But we can listen to the weather forecast too. There is one for inland waterways.'

'But you could get caught out. You know, one time your granda went out on a rowing boat from Maghery. We were waiting for him and he nearly drowned because of the weather. There was a storm and we were standing watching him fighting for his life, pulling and pulling on the oars, the boat going up and down. I thought it was going to turn over. He nearly drowned. He nearly drowned.'

So that was it: bad memories. The place was dangerous in their minds. There were in fact other reasons to stay away from the shore. Sand was removed as a resource for building purposes. You could be enjoying a lovely paddle to cool your feet off in the summer, then disappear down a sandhole you didn't know about. It has happened. Since my Dad had hauled sand for a local building company he knew stopping for a paddle was life threatening. So my parents unspoken logic was 'stay away'.

There was other entertainment on the drive around the north of the orchard county into rural Tyrone in late spring. We could be hit by a swarm of black lough flies that was so dense that we'd think someone had blacked out the sun. Worse was the windscreen suddenly covered in blood as the flies made impact. Daddy stopped the car and we waited. Mummy had shouted a warning a few minutes before in a sort of jolly way – 'Oh, look at that!' – trying to dissipate any panic as she pointed towards a giant black cloud the size of the *Titanic*. So we sat in the back of the car until it passed, fascinated, not scared, even though it was black and there was blood and the flies were hitting the car like hail. Then there was light again and my dad got out of the car to ask for a bucket of water to clean the windscreen. As he did we could see the occupants of the cottages in Maghery leaning over their gates, huddled in groups, pausing while the storm passed. Then they went back to cutting their hedges or whatever they were doing. It was no big deal, it just got in their way for a few minutes. It happened every year, still does – you can still drive into a black-fly storm if you are going round that way now, although the experience is less spectacular because the flies have suffered as a result of pollution and their numbers are sadly diminished.

When did the fishing stop there? I have no idea, but there came a day when the nets were hung up to dry and no one took them down again. On that same drive, year after year, I watched the nets deteriorate. Big holes appeared, bits blew off. In the end they looked like those prayer flags in the Himalayas – shredded bits of weathered fabric, discoloured and flapping about in the wind. A prayer to the past and a prayer of thanks for my grandad being saved from drowning.

That was the far road. On that particular Sunday, we took a different route, setting out along the road that preceded the M1 between The Birches and Dungannon. It sat on top of peat that was about as secure as icing on a cake with an elephant sitting on it. It may have followed the route of an esker – as a child I had no idea about such things, but I loved the drive through the old peatlands full of willow and peat stacks, and the light gauge railway that crossed the road. There were no traffic lights so my father just had to keep a lookout. The driver waved as he chugged by with his long train of peat.

The road turned right to Coalisland, just over the Blackwater River, and continued high above the bogland, saved from flooding by its height. Turning left in

Coalisland, we made the final climb up the stony lane to the top of the precipice where Aunt Lynn's whitewashed thatched cottage welcomed us. Not so welcoming was the outside loo closer to the edge where the old cars were shoved over. Stuff of nightmares. I had to decide between the dangers of peeing outside behind a bush with one of Joe's horses watching or sitting on a wooden frame over a bucket worrying about either falling down the slope or someone opening the door for there was no lock. The horse won every time.

The women were all set for a debate about the Swiss roll, so we children were told to go and play. 'Stay away from that slope! Don't get dirty. Don't light any fires!'

The neighbours' twelve-year-old son arrived driving a tractor to borrow some farm thing. He jumped off the seat and went to search for it in the barn with the men. I remember being insanely jealous that someone so close to me in age had been given this level of freedom. He had driven the long way round, a mile and a half, and would return the same way with the necessary implement, a bill hook. The normally friendly lad ignored us tractorless children for he had entered a new higher plane of existence, that of tractor-driving men. I thought about asking him if I could return with him to get a go on the vehicle – there would be no objections from the adults for this is what you did on farms – but since he had ignored me, I stuck my nose in the air as he took a final lap round in the tractor to make sure we were watching, and chased a hen instead.

'Take us to feed the horse, Uncle Joe,' was the request

from my sister, who was not as affected by the tractor-driving youth as I was.

'Right, let's get some grass and go and see if your Aunt Lynn has a carrot.'

Having had too many close encounters with the horse, who was inclined to breathe over my shoulder when I was having a pee outside, I decided instead to join the Swiss roll debate.

I came in at the cream stage of the discussion.

'Well, Sarah would never have been worried about putting fresh cream in a Swiss roll,' said my grandmother, whose sister (Aunt Sarah) had been head cook at a big house.

'Yes, but Mummy, if Joe goes for a carton of cream it will have gone off in this heat by the time he gets back.'

'What about buttercream, then? Or custard cream?'

'Buttercream is too heavy and we haven't done custard cream yet in the class.'

My mother jumped in. 'And how would you get it rolled up with cream on it?'

'Well, you have to roll it up with a sheet of greaseproof paper inside until it's cool, unroll it, fill it with the beaten cream, then roll it up again.'

'Would you put jam in it as well?'

'Yes, to stop the cream soaking in. And another thing, if it had cream, it wouldn't keep to the next day.'

She must be joking, I thought. There's no chance of a scrap being left. And for goodness' sake let's stop arguing about the rolling and filling – let's start tasting.

'Do you want me to make ham sandwiches?' I asked in

an attempt to move things in the right direction.

My mother suddenly jumped up and went to the window. 'Is that smoke over there? See if that wee fellah' – my five-year-old brother and budding pyromaniac – 'has lit a fire there'll be no Swiss roll.'

I ran outside like a demon for this fire had to be put out or at least blamed on somebody else, maybe the farm next door. Swinging round to the top field I could see Uncle Joe near the plume of smoke in the usual bonfire spot where he burnt rubbish. I ran back in.

'It's just Joe burning the rubbish. That's okay, isn't it?'

My grandmother replied, 'It's Sunday, you don't work on a Sunday, the Lord says.'

'The Lord says Susan is going to make the ham sandwiches, Heather is going to set the table and I'm going to slice the Swiss roll!' replied my aunt.

And shortly afterwards we sat down at the crisp white linen-covered table with creamy milk in the jug and enough sugar for us all to have at least three spoonfuls in each of our numerous cups of tea. There were also beautiful ham sandwiches and the gingerbread made by me, as well as a plate of sliced wheaten bread and a plate of soda farls. After we'd spread at least quarter of an inch of butter on either bread we had the choice of jam or cheese to put on it. For a laugh Joe had both on a soda. The teapot bubbled away on the cooker and was refilled a couple of times to wash everything down. In pride of place was the most delicious Swiss roll I have ever tasted.

There were eight of us so Aunt Lynn cut it into exactly

eight slices saying that she'd do a fresh cream version for next week.

'Can I help?' I asked.

'Why not? Sure get your dad to run you up on Friday evening.'

So the next week he did and I got to go on my own. I am glad I did – filling a Swiss roll with fresh cream is involved and does not need to be complicated by constant advice from those who have never done it, namely my mother and Nanny Wylie. The egg sponge mixture has to be cooked to perfection on a lined baking tray, for if it is too dry then it will crack along the edges when it is rolled. As soon as the sponge is cooked it has to be tipped out of the tin and rolled up in greaseproof paper and left to cool completely. Then it should be filled with whipped cream as close as possible to the time when you're going to serve it. I loved this glimpse into the bakery world, which made me keener than ever to learn as much as possible about cookery. However, a Swiss roll filled with fresh cream is best left to bakeries, I have concluded – to make them at home is too much bother, too much can go wrong, and life is too short.

It was September and I wondered what Sunday's agenda would be: walk or work. The walk tended to be a three-hour hike across the fields belonging to whoever we were visiting. This activity could be classed as the closest to leisure that my family got: I never visited any rural relative where people sat about the place, except when it was time to eat. There were always animals to be fed, logs to be chopped, fields to be checked and hens to be shooed into their houses in the evening so that the fox wouldn't get them. As Sunday was the official day of rest, the pace was a little slower, but my overwhelming memory of rural family and friends is of people being active. Much of the men's socialising was done outdoors, leaning on fences and gates. Women socialised a bit on their way to the shops, or in the shops, but if they called to visit someone, they fell in with whatever needed to be done – fuelling the stove, drying the dishes, bringing in the washing and, most often, baking.

That particular Sunday turned out to be a rare visit to Aunt Maud's, one of my father's sisters. We children sat quietly in our Sunday clothes, as per expectations, as the adults caught up on family news, even though we were busting to get outside and explore because we were seldom at this house. 'You make jam don't you, Heather?' asked Aunt Maud. 'What about plum jam? Have you ever made that?'

'Haven't for a while. Just made strawberry so far – Uncle Frank had a field full in July and didn't get them all sold.'

'Well would you like some plums? Come and see this.'

This looked like permission to run outside so we trooped out along with the adults. The plum tree was taller than the house; its branches drooping with golden-red fruits. We all stood and stared at what seemed to have the potential to become a ton of jam.

'What are you going to do with all of that?' asked my dad, looking at enough fruit to provide for the entire neighbourhood.

'You take a couple of pounds for now and I'll see who else comes round. Get them youngsters up the tree. I'll get some baskets.'

We took off up the tree like squirrels. First job before Aunt Maud came back with the baskets was to see who could get to the top. We managed to get above the roof of the house before the tree started to sway. Aunt Maud's house was on the edge of extensive boglands, connecting the apple-growing edge of Armagh to Lough Neagh. Much of this land is drained now and converted into agricultural acreage, although on the far side of the Blackwater from my aunt's house, part of the bog is conserved as Peatlands Park. From three-quarters of the way up the plum tree I could see across Lough Neagh to the Sperrins, which were lit up in golden sunlight, maybe glowing from the gold that's locked into the rocks there. Closer to where we were, I thought I could see Killyman, where my maternal grandmother lived. I could certainly make out the red glow rising from the brick kilns that were forever lit on the Coalisland Road until about 1965 when brick-making became automated in a factory and the men no longer had to stack the red bricks into the outdoor facilities.

'Daddy, look! I can see Napoleon's Nose on Cavehill! I can see Belfast from here.'

'Can you, right enough? Can you see Uncle George as well up in Joanmount?'

'Don't be silly, Daddy!'

'What about the zoo?'

I started to squint, just in case, but then realised that

Daddy really must be joking. By now my brother was stuffing plums into his mouth like they were going out of fashion. He stopped when Aunt Maud reappeared out of the house with three baskets and we scrambled down to collect them. I don't believe I've ever seen such a crop of plums since. The baskets were filled in a matter of minutes and passed down to the adults. I was hot and thirsty and looking forward to a cup of tea.

Aunt Maud called up the tree to us, 'Help yourselves before you come in for your tea.'

Perfectly ripe plums, the same temperature as a sunny autumn afternoon, straight off the branch, are the food of the gods, and I was in my child-heaven, looking down from my plum-tree perch. I slept well and dreamt well that night – and had many weeks of plum jam sandwiches in my school lunchbox.

Gingerbread

8oz (200g) flour
½ tsp baking powder
½ tsp ground ginger
¼ tsp ground cinnamon
½ tsp salt
2oz (50g) demerara sugar
2oz (50g) raisins
4oz (100g) crystalised ginger
3oz (75g) butter
1 tbsp golden syrup

1 tbsp treacle
1 egg
¼ pint (125ml) buttermilk
1oz (25g) flaked almonds

Grease and line a medium-sized loaf tin. Heat the oven to 180°C.

Sieve the flour, baking powder, spices and salt into a bowl. Stir in the sugar, dried fruit and ginger.

Heat the butter, syrup, treacle and buttermilk gently untl they blend, then add, along with the egg, to the dry ingredients in the bowl. Mix well.

Pour the mixture into the loaf tin, sprinkle with the almonds and bake for 45 minutes or until a skewer inserted into the gingerbread comes out clean.

6

Beef Tea

'Beef tea, that's what he needs,' said Aunt Lynn, looking into a gallon-sized aluminium soup pot. 'It'll take all day, he'll have to wait.' The steam rose around her face, across the low pine-clad scullery ceiling, out over the top of the peeling green half-door to the back garden where I was contemplating climbing an old apple tree. With the hearing prowess of a bat I never missed anything. I also knew where the conversation was going.

'Well, I don't know about that,' came the reply from my grandmother. 'Anyway, how do you know what you're doing?'

'What do you mean?'

'Who told you how to make beef tea?'

'Aunt Sarah.'

'Did she tell you it had to simmer for at least a day?'

'Yes! Isn't that what I just said?'

Entertainment over, and with the same dignity as usual, my grandmother went to inspect a row of cabbages in the vegetable patch. She could supervise the beef tea and make sure it was up to standard later on.

I hopped and skipped down the three steps from the back garden on to the cement backyard. The steps were opposite my aunt and uncle's bedroom. I hadn't seen my uncle all day, which was unusual for a Saturday, so I decided to upturn a galvanised bucket which was sitting conveniently beside the water butt, stand on it and have a look through the open bedroom window to find out more. First I had to ascertain my aunt's whereabouts. She had left the kitchen and was somewhere else in the house. Good. It's very difficult not to make a noise with a clanging metal bucket but I did my best. Between the bucket and the bit of height I had aged eight, and clasping the window ledge to pull myself up, I could see my uncle lying motionless in bed. If I could just get a foothold, I could get a knee up on the ledge and ask him what was wrong.

Kneeling on the windowsill, I shouted through the open window, 'Joe, what's wrong with you?'

'Right! Get down this minute.'

I obeyed by toppling off the bucket on to my backside.

'What were you doing up on the window ledge?'

'I was worried about Joe.'

'He's not well, and so don't wake him up!'

'Is that why you're making beef tea? Can I have a look?'

This involved standing on top of a cushion on top of a three-legged stool. The galvanised bucket may have been more secure, but it was not tall enough. Inside the steaming pot was a shin bone and several hunks of meat. The boiling liquor was flecked with bits of brown – some of the grains of meat had started to flake off. Golden globules of fat floated around like planets. It smelt kind of okay.

I decided to chance it. 'Can I taste it?'

My aunt took a china mug off one of the hooks on the shelf that ran the length of the scullery and over the doorway into the living room. Well out of reach for me. It was also the location of the biscuit tin. It was always full of biscuits, but that was not my priority right now. Here also were the cake tins, a preserving pan and a stash of home-made jams. The jam jars were all misted up with the steam from the boiling beef tea, demonstrating that the scullery was several degrees colder than the rest of the house. She took the soup ladle from the top drawer, fished around the giant pot trying to avoid globules of golden fat and floating bits of marrow and large lumps of meat, then gave me half a cup. Still standing on the three-legged stool, I clasped the cup carefully in both hands, blew across the surface and took a little girl sip, with my shoulders hunched up. I liked standing up here, I was in the adult world at their level, on equal terms.

'Mmmm ...'

'Well?'

'I think I would like some salt in it.'

Out came the blue tub of salt. A pinch of salt went into the cup, and a toss into the meat liquor. I liked the taste, but knew this was it. This was some sort of home remedy entirely devoted to the revival of my uncle. I was not sick and therefore not entitled to anything but a taste. And Joe must have been really ill for I never knew him to take to his bed before or since.

'Could I have a bit of bread to dip into it?' I asked, climbing down.

My aunt sliced off the heel of a batch loaf for me. She lathered it with the standard quarter inch of butter and handed it to me. Steam rose off the beef tea as I raised to my lips. I nearly wished I was sick to get this treat.

'See when I had mumps, Aunt Lynn. Mummy didn't make this.'

There was no answer to this and my aunt disappeared into the living room from where Joe was now shouting for a cup of leaf tea. I sat with my elbows on the plastic table cloth swinging my legs under the table with the china cup in both hands, making the beef tea last for as long as I could.

At the scullery table I thought about the mumps, me lying in bed for a week, the crushing headache and the inability to swallow. I could hear my friends playing outside and the rapid slapping of the skipping rope. My mother would go out for messages, with headscarf and shopping basket, and toddler in tow, and the girls would run up to the front door and ask, 'Mrs Farrell, is Susan all right? When is she coming out to play?'

'The doctor said it will be two weeks until she's better.'

'Two weeks! Oh my God!'

'Don't say "Oh my God", Sally. You're not supposed to,' said Angela, the oldest.

Sally said 'Oh my God' again for badness.

'Right, girls, I'm away to the shops. See you later.'

I could hear them whispering at my front door. Usually in this situation I would be calling out the bedroom window to them. Or they would all be invited in, and they would all tumble up the stairs to see me and have a nosy at the same time. But nobody wanted mumps, and I couldn't even lift my head off the pillow, and I wasn't sure if I was dreaming or awake, for my friends' whispers seemed to be right beside my bed. But it was only my mother back again, asking if I would try and drink a cup of tea and eat a biscuit. 'You could dip it in the tea and it will go real soft.'

I sat up and decided to have a go. I was propped up with three feather pillows and a towel was tucked under my chin for safety purposes. I took a few sips of the tepid sweet tea. It felt like swallowing a mouthful of pins. But not just as bad as the last time I tried.

'No biscuit, thank you.'

The over-sweetened tea slid down, nearly cold but reviving.

'I want to get up.'

'No – the doctor says to stay where you are.'

The doctor and my mother were right: when I lay down again I still couldn't work out if my friends' whispers were in the room or outside in the front garden. I woke up in the dark and wondered where they were and shouted for them. My mother arrived like Florence Nightingale with rollers. She offered me an aspirin crushed and mixed with jam from a dessert spoon and we argued about my taking it. We compromised on another cup of sweet tepid tea, which washed it down. Next thing I knew there was another cup of tea and the curtains were open. My neck didn't feel so bad and I looked less like Hammy Hamster.

My mother must have heard me moving around as

she appeared with a steaming bowl of tapioca, complete with a large blob of jam in the middle. There are two types of tapioca, small grain and large grain. Large grain is about the same size as frogspawn and many would claim it tastes very similar – except I don't believe they have actually tasted it. My mother presented me with the smaller-grain variety and I carefully took a small mouthful. I liked it okay, but I was worried about the pain of swallowing. That morning, thankfully, it felt more like having my throat tickled than being stabbed with a million pins. However I reckoned a fry was a good few days' away yet.

Jam was one my mother's favourite 'building-up' ingredients when any of us were sick. It went down easily, disguised all manner of medicines and there were always plentiful supplies. The doctor had advised her: 'Get lots of sweet things into those children, keep their energy up, something like jam, Mrs Farrell.' He knew her well enough to know ours was a sweet-free and lemonade-free household except at party time. There were worse things than jam. Had I been sick in my grandmother's house, panada would have been on the menu. Panada is a kind of soup of bits of bread boiled in milk with a good few spoonfuls of sugar. It should not be too runny, about the thickness of a milk pudding such as baked rice or even tapioca. It slips down wonderfully well.

Jam in quantity reappeared on the menu when I got a dose of food poisoning. It came on me in Primary 7. I suddenly felt really peculiar and threw up on the classroom floor. The caretaker was sent for with his bucket of sawdust to take care of the boke and I was sent home, a mile walk on my own. No more boking in the classroom, thank you. I believe I may have been the first child to achieve the four-minute mile. Even then, in the midst of my anxiety about getting home, I had the vague thought that I shouldn't have been dispatched from school like this. It has only taken fifty years to work out that it was very wrong indeed.

I got myself home on sheer willpower, collapsing through the front door under the usual cross-examination of 'Why are you back from school?' It became obvious very quickly. I remember the doctor calling every day, and waking up every night screaming. I heard the doctor say something like, 'We'll see how it goes over the next twenty-four hours.' What did that mean? Twenty-four hours and I would be in the funeral parlour? Or was it twenty-four hours and he would send me to hospital? In fact, in twenty-four hours I was sitting outside in the garden being given ice cream with jam in it, of course. I was in the company of my grandmother and aunt, who must have been sent for, as they would only emerge from south Tyrone/north Armagh for births, deaths and marriages and the visits of long-lost overseas relatives they didn't expect to see ever again.

Their visit involved my father, in his bread delivery van, calling with my grandmother, his mother-in-law, to ask her to come to Portadown because the doctor had said that the next twenty-four hours would tell the tale about Susan, who had come home very ill from school the other day. He asked her to get in touch with Aunt Lynn too. My grandfather cycled the five miles to Aunt Lynn's to tell her she needed to get to Portadown fast, and could she go with her mother because the bus for Portadown via Maghery went past the end of their lane. So then my aunt cycled the five miles back with her father, and caught the bus with her mother.

As we sat in the garden, the next I knew I was being offered *extra ice cream*. What? Extra ice cream? I had never been offered a second helping of ice cream in my life, so I asked why.

'Oh, the doctor said you needed to build yourself up.'

'Actually I don't want any more, thanks.' The ice cream was sickly sweet – I have avoided raspberry ripple to this day. Taste buds still out of action, I remember saying I wanted to go back to bed and being followed upstairs by everyone wanting to know why I didn't want some more ice cream, demanding, 'Is there something wrong with you?'

Thank God I was only a child and still had the ability to drift off into a deep sleep at the drop of a hat, in this case listening to the adults arguing about how they were going to get more ice cream and jam into me. I believe I might have said something like 'I'll take a cup of tea and toast later' before I went unconscious to get them out of my room. And so I did – toast with my grandmother's strawberry jam sitting up in bed in the gathering darkness, the extended family away on the last Dungannon bus. I was glad we had no fridge and that the ghastly raspberry ripple could not be saved for another day. It must have been eaten by someone else – likely the dog, who had entirely undiscriminating tastes.

Beef tea would have been appropriate in my situation. It comes under the heading of 'Invalid cookery', well documented by Mrs Beeton and available as part of a training course through St John Ambulance when I was young. I was a cadet in the charity in 1967. This was a junior branch of the organisation, all girls. We studied first aid, basic nursing skills and did formation marches to military music in the canteen of a sewing factory off Thomas Street in Portadown on a Tuesday night. I hold a certificate from them for 'Home Nursing', a course that included invalid cookery. This type of cookery comes from a time when there was no health service and people had to take care of their own illnesses. Particular types of food were believed to be healing and restorative, and so they were. Try boiling a whole chicken in a deep pot, season well and throw in a couple of spoonfuls of barley. This stock, well skimmed, will quell a queasy stomach. Your body will soak up the nutrients and you will start to feel like yourself again. In the Indian tradition, a spoonful of turmeric is added at the start of the process. Moving towards Iran, dried mint is added. This is my favourite one for queasiness and recovery. Chicken stock including barley, mint and turmeric works like magic; it is soothing and easy to digest.

Lurgan Hospital also had a really good invalid food

philosophy. When I went to get my tonsils out we had compulsory ice cream every day. They believed that children should be fed every two hours, and who was I to disagree?

Later in life, following chemotherapy, invalid cookery became important to me again. I went on to a nutritional programme to strengthen my badly weakened digestive system. Shin beef was back on the menu as a base for life-sustaining broth. Chicken stock with mint and turmeric was, at times, the only thing I could keep down. It soothed my severely challenged internal organs and got nutrients into my blood. The nutritionists I met on a course at the Haven Breast Cancer Centre in Fulham, London, found the idea of invalid cookery really funny when I mentioned it to them, but this is what they were teaching: they were advising us to make and use foods that were easy to digest, as well as being light, tasty and sustaining. Whatever they called it, their great enthusiasm gave me comfort in some very dark days, for what my ancestors and the ancients of Iran and India had known about food for centuries had been thoroughly researched and endorsed, and put back on the menu.

The easy way to produce the recipes below is to invest in a slow cooker. Many people have one secreted away in the back of a kitchen cupboard. Get it out. For a busy household with people out working all day it's invaluable. You can pop a joint of meat in it in the morning and when you come home from work, there is the most delicious smell as you open the door. The meat is cooked nicely, flaking and only needing something on the side.

Chicken Stock

Place the chicken carcass in a large saucepan with 2–3 pints (1.1–1.7 litres) of water, 1 teaspoon salt and 2 tablespoons of barley. Bring to the boil and then turn down the heat and simmer gently for an hour or two until the barley is quite soft. Taste it to see if you need to adjust the seasoning. Strain through a sieve.

You can use the resulting stock for a variety of things – soup, risotto, curry or, my favourite, noodle soup. You won't believe how delicious this is. Add an inch (2½cm) of chopped fresh root ginger, a chopped clove of garlic, a couple of chopped scallions and a julienned carrot or two to the stock. Cook for about five minutes before adding a handful or two or thin egg noodles. When the noodles are soft, it's ready. Other good additions are sliced mushrooms, spinach and frozen peas. If I am making soup with the stock I always add a teaspoon of dried mint towards the end of the process.

Beef Tea

1 good-sized piece of shin of beef
1 tsp turmeric
1 tsp salt
½ tsp white pepper
2 stalks of celery, washed and chopped
1 onion, peeled and chopped
1 large carrot, peeled and sliced

Put everything into a slow cooker with a couple of pints of water and leave for at least eight hours, maybe overnight, at the lowest setting. Strain the resulting liquor into a saucepan – this is your beef tea or stock.

To make broth, add Buchanan's soup mix, together with soup vegetables like chopped leek, parsley, carrot and celery. Soup mix is pearl barley, red lentils and green split peas, packed by Buchanan's, a Northern Ireland-based company that has been around for over a hundred years.

If you're using either of these recipes to make soup for someone who is ill, you must skim off the fat before liquidising the soup.

7

High Days and Holy Days

Usually we didn't have visitors for Christmas – it was more often a low-key affair with stockings in the morning and then Christmas lunch. So the year when Aunty Bessie, dressed in her fur coat, entered our decked-out living room as if she were the queen, was very special. Aunty Bessie stood and smiled at us with her handbag over one arm and a shopping bag full of presents over the other. In her hands she very carefully held a deep, square cake tin. It was her home-baked Christmas cake, weighing half a stone – her contribution to the festivities.

My mother carefully took the cake and placed it on the dining table – set out for the occasion in the living room – among the crackers and the good cutlery. She prised off the tight lid and the Christmas aroma floated out and all around the room and everyone seemed to take it in and smile. I looked in the tin, down on to a winter wonderland – peaks of snow, a mini Christmas tree, a snowman with a scarf and hat and Rudolf the red-nosed reindeer. I put my hand in to test the icing. 'Hang on, hang on, that's for later,' said my mum, as Aunty Bessie just smiled. But I was happy – I had found out that the icing had the same consistency as ice. Only not freezing cold. Amazing!

With the exception of my father, Christmas in our family seemed to be mainly for women and children, for the next to arrive were Aunt Lynn and Nanny Wylie, laden with packages and tins. Christmas was about to settle down in proper order. Those parcels were for us kids and right now I was torn between enjoying the delicious smells coming out of the kitchen and wondering what was in such large packages. We'd definitely have to eat before I was allowed to open them, and there'd be tea before that – perhaps sherry. It took me until I was over fifty to realise that not everyone expects tea when they arrive for Christmas dinner. A distant relative asked me if I was joking when I offered her a cup one Christmas morning in middle England. No, dear lady, I was not.

Finally it was nearly dinner time. My dad took the enormous foil-covered turkey out of the oven and then made the gravy with Bisto and some of the juices from the pan. My mum and my aunt mashed the potatoes, and then the carrots and parsnips with plenty of butter and a bit of milk. Then they drained the sprouts. They plated the veg in the kitchen and we all squeezed around the table with our steaming plates in front of us, waiting for Dad to carve and serve the turkey.

We pulled our crackers, ate our dinner in silly paper hats … and finally it was time to open our presents. My job was to hand them out because I could read. Big baby dolls kitted out in hand-knitted clothes for me and my sister. A trike for my brother. Pyjamas, slippers and socks for all. Aunty Bessie got us annuals, *The Beano* for me, Disney for my sister and Andy Pandy for my brother.

Aunt Lynn got a large box of Milk Tray, and Aunty Bessie a large Black Magic, very large, the size of a tea tray, from someone called Santa. The Milk Tray had a Canadian snow scene on the lid. The Black Magic had an elaborately tied red ribbon at a jaunty angle, set off against the black packaging, tasteful and elegant just like Aunty Bessie. They would need help with the contents. So we helped.

I ended the day cosied up under an eiderdown quilt, two wool blankets and carefully ironed cotton sheets; cuddled up to my baby doll, both of us in our new jammies; a hot water bottle at my feet; and some Black Magic under my pillow, in case I needed some magic in the middle of the night. Which of course I would.

The best and only place for Easter – and I'm talking about the chocolate egg part, when the holy part was over – was Aunt Lynn's. The church part was sort of okay, from the point of view that the arrival of Easter was a signal for new clothes: lighter for the forthcoming warmer weather and bigger for the unavoidable growth patterns of children. I was taken on my own for my fit-out of new shoes (always white), new ankle socks, white again, a hat and gloves. The dresses and cardigans were home-made and magically appeared out of nowhere, or so it seemed to me until I was eleven and started sewing my own dresses. This was fine by me as it meant that I could now go and pick my dress pattern and fabric in Corbett's department store in Portadown.

I loved going to Corbett's – it felt very grown up. It

was a double-fronted department store, with curved glass windows on both sides of the entrance doors. A lot of our clothes were made either by my mother or her friend Edna (Mrs Anderson to us), so the trip to the fabric department at the back of the store was one I made often from when I was a small child until I learnt to sew for myself. During my childhood, there were always prams with babies in them parked outside the shop – this was the standard practice.

I remember a particular hat that sat on top of my head with a small brim and flowers attached to the band. Did it rain any Easter whatsoever when I was growing up to ruin this style? No, it did not. Nor did it rain in the summer holidays – only once when we were in a caravan in Millisle. The rainy years started in the eighties.

After eating our Easter lunch, we were up the road for the Easter egg search at Aunt Lynn and Uncle Joe's. A barn, a hen house, a tool shed, a pig house, the back field, the front garden, the side garden and the orchard all needed a fingertip search. There were usually three eggs each, left by the Easter bunny. Disputes arose when one of us thought an egg belonging to someone else was better than the one meant for us. We spent a long time searching every cobwebby outhouse corner, every hole in the hedge, and every crook of every apple tree in white shoes, socks and cardigans, trying not to get anything dirty (usually we didn't). If one of us came in crying because we had found two eggs and not three like the others, then the men would emerge from the fireplace and drag themselves outside, smoking and laughing. They'd start shouting and pointing, 'Hotter, hotter! No, you're going cold now,' or simply reach the egg down from the pear tree for my brother – usually the child crying – as he was the smallest and he was never going to be able to reach it anyway.

When we were summoned in from the fields, I washed my hands with the Lifebuoy soap which was the size of a brick – the smell of it would have killed germs at fifty feet.

'Hurry up, we are all waiting on you,' said my mother from the living room, for the Easter tea was formal and the fold-out table had been put in the centre of the room, covered in a white tablecloth and the best china. I sat down beside my grandmother on the stool which was really a sewing box with tiny legs. A cushion had been placed on top so that I could reach the table. Our Easter eggs were displayed on the sideboard. I had a Bachelors one – I loved to sing their hits. I knew by looking at my brother's Mickey Mouse egg that he had eaten half of it and tried to conceal the crime by (badly) reshaping the foil.

The last plate was put on the table in front of me: scrambled eggs, ham and tomato. All tomatoes in Aunt Lynn's house were skinned, for she had a fear of choking. Why she skinned everyone's tomatoes I will never know, as she was the only one afraid of choking. I reached for the pepper.

'Don't reach across the table,' said my mother. 'Say "Please pass the pepper" to whoever is nearest.'

'Okay. Please pass the pepper, Daddy.'

'What about the mustard?' Uncle Joe asked me. 'Do you take mustard on your ham? Go on try a wee bit.' He put quarter of a teaspoon on the edge of my plate.

'You will have to eat that now,' said Nanny Wylie, firmly – unless it was poisonous, anything on the plate in front of you had to be eaten. I considered my strategy. I knew that the mustard was a joke set up by Joe to provide some Easter entertainment, but I was used to eating whatever was offered and mainly liked the new things I tried. Last week, however, my sister had accidentally taken a bite from a ham and mustard sandwich – she had missed the telltale yellow staining on the bread, and she squealed at the shock of the unexpected heat.

I was determined to get the mustard down without flinching, so I came up with a plan. Step 1, ask politely to have the bread plate passed my way so I could put a slice of ham and the mustard inside a soda farl. Step 2, make sure my tea is at the right temperature. Step 3, make sure I have a neutral expression on my face or better one of innocence, like a lamb to a mustard slaughter. Step 4, hold the ham-and-mustard soda farl up to my mouth and make sure Joe is watching, which, of course, he was. In fact most people were looking at me: Nanny Wylie to make sure I was eating the mustard, Aunt Lynn and mother because they were familiar with Joe's humour, and my brother and sister because everyone else was watching.

I took a bite, chewed very deliberately, licked my lips and asked, 'Mummy, can I always have mustard on my ham sandwiches for school?'

'We'll see.' She thought she knew better, but I have loved mustard ever since, and the hotter the better.

My sister's eyes were watering as I took the last corner of the bread, cleaned the mustard off my plate with it and popped it in my mouth. Joe offered her the mustard pot, so she slid under the table. I took a big gulp of tea out of the gold-rimmed china cup and politely asked for a refill. I followed the soda with a piece of gingerbread, a slice of wheaten with last year's damson jam and a bun, and then waited patiently for a large wedge of the Easter Victoria sandwich, and another cup of tea. The mustard fire was well and truly extinguished and I didn't even have watery eyes or sneeze, because I enjoyed every bit of it.

Joe was now trying to persuade my brother that if his big sister could eat mustard then so could he, but he was only three so Aunt Lynn finally said, 'Stop codding around, Joe, and drink your tea, or go and study the gee-gees.' So he took his cup and newspaper and a packet of Players and retired to the outside toilet. He would be back in a while to coach us in poker, but only if we had pennies.

'Heather, what recipe did you use for that gingerbread? There's something different about it.'

'I sent away for a Stork margarine cookery book, and got it from there—'

'Margarine! Don't tell me you have been using margarine!' said my grandmother. 'Sarah would never use margarine.'

'Yes, well, I'm not Sarah, and that's what it says in the recipe.'

As the margarine versus butter debate raged on, I ran outside in case there was tidying up for me to do. I preferred to be hanging out of an apple tree. My dad would run Nanny Wylie home soon and then the cards would come out for us – her departure ended the holy part of the day. If we didn't want to play cards then we could stay outside until it was time for us to go home – not too late, though, for we always had a substantial supper before bed, probably a bun and a cup of tea, no matter how much we had eaten during the day.

My fourth birthday party.

In the photograph of my fourth birthday party, we are at the pudding stage. There are bowls of trifle in front of everyone and there are two cakes yet to be demolished

– a chocolate cake with Maltesers and my birthday cake with the frill removed so that I could blow out the candles without setting the place on fire. I am on the right and my friend Noell standing beside me has been shifted to make way for the photographer. This looks like the sort of spread you might expect at a garden party in Buckingham Palace: the tablecloth, the cup and saucer for each child, the crystal sugar bowls and milk jugs, and a large pot of tea for top-ups. None of these cups had anything other than tea in them for tea was all that any of us drank. We probably started the birthday tea with egg sandwiches and wheaten bread but by this stage the sweet part of the menu is definitely outweighing any troublesome directions towards healthy eating.

I am pleased that this excellent tradition of afternoon tea has been re-established, although it can be quite expensive. The most impressive price I have come across was £75 per person at the Ritz in London. Locally, the price is more like £17.50 per person. For us, it was a budget meal as everything was home-made. There was just time and skill involved in the making of the food.

Baking, sewing and knitting were hobbies for my mother and her friend, Mrs Anderson, who was the mother of my friend Noell. Our little cardigans and dresses were all home-made. As well as shopping at Corbett's, my mother had an account in the local wool shop – every knitted item we wore throughout our childhoods, until university and beyond, was handmade from pure wool, a good material when you know how to handle it for it resists stains and can be pressed clean with a damp cloth.

For the birthday feast Mrs Anderson made my dress. My mother took me round to her house at the final stage of sewing and I stood on the table for the hem to be pinned. A very prickly experience for the pins sometimes came into contact with my legs, but I was made to stand on the table until the hem was straight enough to meet Mrs Anderson's approval. No need for a spirit level – Mrs Anderson's eyes were as sure as anything. She also had a special ruler that sat upright on the tabletop, enabling her to double check that the hem was the same at the front and at the back. The ruler had a shorter straight-edged piece of wood that could be slid up and down to the desired length. I slowly turned in a circle so they could examine the hem against the measure. 'Mummy, can I get down, please?' I asked. I had seen Mrs Anderson's son Paul carry a large can outside. Earlier he had sworn to me that there was a newt in it. His plan was to dig a pond in the back garden and recreate a suitable environment for this mysterious creature that I had never heard of. Of course I was invited to help with the digging under his supervision. There was the matter of the white shoes and ankle socks I was wearing but I would worry about that later.

'Hang on, we're nearly finished. Another couple of pins.'

I closed my eyes tight and covered them with my hands in anticipation of a jag.

'Stand still! You'll get a pin in your leg if you move.'

I froze, and there was no jag – they were careful enough and did not want blood on my hem. I was not sure if I was happy about this or not, for part of the afternoon would be spent comparing the scratches on my knees with those on Noell's after we'd had a look at the newt.

'Right ya-girl-ya, away you go and change. Give the dress to Mrs Anderson and away outside and play. We'll call you in when it's time for tea.'

Oh good, I thought, for the kitchen still had the aroma of fairy cakes. Could I grab one on the way through? I expected Paul had already taken a cake and so maybe he would get the blame for both if I snaffled one as well. I decided that I could hold on; I would rather eat it at the table with a cup of tea. There would be dozens as my mother and Mrs Anderson had made enough for the two households for the week, to cover supper and lunchboxes and anyone who dropped in. It would never do to run out of buns.

Without fail, any family gathering like my birthday involved egg sandwiches and cake. The other occasion for such a spread would be a visit from relatives, in particular those who had travelled a long way, from England or even further afield, who would do the rounds and could expect to get similar fare in the household of each part of the family. As well as the egg sandwiches, standards for the table were ham sandwiches and a Madeira cake or Victoria sponge. Madeira cake was boring to me as a child – I couldn't see the point of a cake without a creamy filling or at least icing on top. I decided it was for elderly people after overhearing aged aunts saying that such a cake would keep in a tin for at least two weeks. Whoever heard of 'keeping' a cake?

A spread like this was laid on for the visit of our first cousins, the Hodgetts, who needed a proper meal, having travelled halfway around the world (from Preston in England). They were staying with Aunt Sarah in Ballynakelly and had come to visit us in our prefab in Portadown. There was an individual salad plated for each person – lettuce, tomato, ham, boiled egg and beetroot – followed by trifle and Victoria sponge. There was always soda or wheaten bread on the side for anyone who fancied it and as an insurance policy to make sure that everyone was properly full. I have come to believe that most of my cells are made of soda bread because I ate so much of it as a child.

The Preston folk had been away from Ireland for a long time so these home-made breads went down very well indeed. The cousins did themselves proud. 'Please, Aunty Heather,' asked Gail, the older and bolder, 'could you pass me another piece of soda bread?'

'You must like that damson jam too, Gail,' observed Aunt Lynn, who had made the jam and was pleased.

'Still plenty of damson bushes?' asked Aunty Minnie, who was my grandmother's sister and hadn't seen a damson or a damson bush since she had left the homeplace for Preston many years before.

'Oh yes, the hedges around Derryvale are full of them,' replied Aunt Lynn.

'There were none last year; it must have been a late frost. Evelyn, how old exactly is that jam?' asked my grandmother. We all knew what was coming now.

'It's on the label!' retorted Lynn. She lifted the jar and

studied the label but didn't say anything.

'Let me see,' said my grandmother, half-smiling, for this was a tease.

She began to search her black leather snap-shut pre-war handbag (very good quality, cream-coloured leather lining with silk inner pockets, some now torn) for my granda's reading glasses. At about this time my granda would have been sitting at home in front of the fire anticipating doing the football pools. After stoking the fire until it was roaring, he would have stood up to get out his pools paperwork and his Bic biro, black for clarity. He needed to fill in the little pink boxes on the form, and they were very hard to make out without reading glasses. He would then have returned to his armchair beside the fire, lit a Player's cigarette then reached down between the cushion and side of his chair to get his glasses case. Unfortunately for him, they were, at that moment, some eighteen miles away. My grandmother perched the brown tortoiseshell (Bakelite really) reading glasses held together by black insulating tape on her nose and proceeded to read the label on the nearly empty jar.

'1961! That's five years old. That's one of those jars you've been storing on top of the wardrobe!' She put it back on the table with a theatrical 'humpft'. My aunt replied, 'Well, it tastes better after it sits for a couple of years.'

Unaware of the background drama of the adult exchange, Gail reached for the jar, scraped out the last of the jam with the butter knife – definitely not allowed, but nobody was going to check the visitors – and spread it over the quarter-inch-thick layer of butter on her soda farl. She ate it with great deliberation, wiped her fingers on her freshly laundered, pressed and beautifully folded serviette, replaced it on her knee and then scanned the tea table for her next choice now that the five-year-old jam was gone.

Having over-the-water family you are fond of but don't see very much means you want to treat them. So before the Preston gang arrived at our little prefab my mother added a bottle of salad cream to the grocery list. It took pride of place in the middle of the table on the day of the visit, showing that my mother was going to a great deal of trouble to make sure that there was everything on the table that anyone could possibly wish for.

'Would you like some of this?' was not a question usually directed at children fifty-odd years ago. You were given a portion of whatever food was going and thanked the adult who gave it to you. As a child who never refused any food or ever had any fears about new foods, I watched as my mother put several blobs of salad cream over my beloved salad. It smelt really strange, something was not right. I couldn't eat the salad, probably largely because she'd overdone it with the salad cream. It's one of only three foods I hate to this day.

'What's wrong with you? You better eat the salad – you can't have just bread.'

I squirmed and tried to slide under the table. How was I going to get out of this? No one appeared to be paying me any attention except my mother.

'Eat it all up.'

'I don't like the salad cream.'

'Just eat it.'

I scraped as much of the slimy goo off my lettuce and tomatoes as I could, stuffed loads of soda bread into my mouth to take away the taste, then washed it all down with as much tea as I could get into me.

'Make more tea, Heather,' said my dad. 'Susan's drinking it like it's going out of fashion.'

My mother topped up my cup as I watched the cousins clean the salad cream off their plates with bread and pop it in their mouths. What was wrong with them? Still, I hoped they would take more so we would be left with an empty bottle. Until it was all used up, the offending condiment would appear on the table every time we had salad. This could go on for several years, for we had never heard of use by dates. The test was to smell it and if it didn't stink then it was okay. It was already stinking as far as I was concerned. Never mind, I thought, here comes the trifle – it will get rid of the taste. Trifle was actually one of those rare things in our house that my mother made solely from convenience foods: a packet of trifle sponges, a tin of fruit cocktail, jelly, cooled custard, whipped cream and hundreds and thousands.

We had a special trifle set of a large moulded glass bowl with a flower pattern and half a dozen matching serving bowls; one of my parents' wedding presents. Really we needed more bowls, which we never did get sorted, so a couple of people always had to have their trifle on a piece plate. There were tinned strawberries in the trifle that day along with the usual tin of fruit cocktail to ensure there was enough for everyone. I began to recover from the salad cream experience

'Thanks very much, Aunty Heather,' chimed my English cousins. 'That was lovely.'

'Okay girls, take Susan out to play. Don't get your good dresses dirty now, sure you won't?'

I ran out the door hoping the fresh air and some jumping up and down would eliminate any lingering traces of salad cream.

A year later, when I was ten, Aunt Sarah put an announcement round the family that she was going to organise a barbecue for another visit from the Hodgetts.

'What's a barbecue, Mummy?' I asked when the letter came.

'A bonfire for cooking sausages on. You put the sausage in a bridge roll and eat it out of your hand. We'll have baked potatoes as well.'

'Who all is coming?'

'The Hodgetts, Aunt Lila, Ronnie, Uncle Frank, Aunt Lynn, maybe the Hollands, Nanny Wylie.'

Thank goodness for the cousins from Preston, for everyone else was a million years old. But Aunt Sarah's house was good fun because Uncle Frank grew strawberries on a smallholding basis and they were therefore guaranteed to be on the menu. There might even be cream in the cool press outside to go with them. If not, we'd get it from the top of the milk – if the bottles were placed in a bucketful of cold well water, the cream would separate and rise to the top. With careful handling this could be skimmed off and used as pouring cream.

There would be a trifle as well, of course, and there would be salad, egg mayonnaise, potato salad, sliced boiled beetroot set in cherry jelly, and cold roast chicken. Since we'd received the letter, the menu was the sole topic of conversation. We even heard that Aunt Sarah was borrowing tables from the church to set everything out like a buffet.

'What's a buffet, Mummy?'

'All the food is set out on long tables and you just go and help yourself.' This was beginning to sound like heaven to me. I could avoid anything that looked like salad cream and help myself. My friends got sick of listening to me in the week running up to the barbecue.

'Oh here she goes again. "Help yourself! Help yourself!" Who cares?'

Me. I did. It was August so in preparation I picked out my favourite cotton flowery dress, whitened my sandals and set them and my ankle socks on my bedroom chair the night before the adventure.

Next morning I got up early and went down into the larder to check out our contribution to the event. Half a dozen cake tins were piled up in anticipation. I opened each in turn. There was a round of wheaten bread, a chocolate cake with Maltesers on top, two dozen fairy cakes and soda bread. As I opened the last tin and got a waft of gingerbread, made with marmalade by the wonderful smell of it, I heard my dad come down the stairs.

'Your mum is sick. We're not going anywhere today. You'll have to look after her and your brother and sister until I drive up to Ballynakelly and tell your aunt Sarah.' With that he left.

I knew there was no point in crying dramatically – I had tried that before and it had had no effect whatsoever. It wasn't going to change anything and besides, there was no audience. My mother was busy being sick in bed and my younger siblings would have been no more impressed by my tears than the adults. But I had listened in to so much of the anticipation, expectation and elevation of the event, I felt like I had been dropped from a great height. I was going to miss the barbecue, al fresco buffet, the whatever-you-want-to-call-it, that was being prepared by my Aunt Sarah who had the same status as the head cook at Downton and was the go-to person to settle all arguments about food. I needed a cup of tea.

Perfect Tea

Tea is no more just tea than food is just food. My guests will often ask me what tea I use. Lots of people think the answer is in a particular brand but that is not so – there are many factors that contribute to the flavour, including the utensils. One of the best cups of tea I ever had was in a factory canteen. It came from a giant factory teapot; it had a great flavour; it was thirst quenching and reviving; and there were tea leaves in the bottom of the cup.

Equipment
metal teapot (stainless steel, or an old-fashioned tin
  one will do)
china cups – tea tastes better in a china cup or mug
tea strainer
tea cosy

Water should be freshly drawn, not water that has been boiled several times (and lost some of its oxygen). The oxygen in the water is an important component of good tea: it enhances the taste.

Good-quality tea leaves are the secret. Tea bags will never match their flavour for the leaves in the bags are reduced to a dust and, as a result of evaporation, lose some of the essential oils that give the tea its flavour. My favourite tea leaves are S.D. Bell's or Bewleys. Either way, you're looking for a blend that resembles dried leaves as opposed to dust. The type of water you have will affect the taste, so you will have to work out which type of tea leaves best suits your water supply. If you can get water from a well, there will be no chlorine or other chemicals in the water.

Warm the teapot with some boiling water. For each cup of tea, put one teaspoon of tea leaves into the pot, and one extra. Then pour the boiling water on to the leaves.

The old-fashioned way to make tea is to let it draw over a source of heat. S.D. Bell's tea stubbornly refuses to release its full flavour unless it has a little birl on the heat. Alternatively use a tea cosy and leave the pot for five minutes to allow the tea to develop its flavour. The tea is ready when it releases its aroma.

Add fresh milk or a slice of lemon. If you like your tea on the strong side, like me, lemon will not compensate for the extra tannin as milk does. If you drink your tea light, lemon is a nice alternative to milk.

I will not tell you whether or not to put milk in first. There are many arguments about this. I put the milk in first as I believe it sinks the tea leaves. You can also use a strainer, although I don't do this as I think that the leaves continue to work their magic in the cup.

Add sugar to taste.

8

School Holidays

In 1968, we rented a cottage in Ballymartin, a village between Kilkeel and Annalong in County Down. I was twelve. One afternoon, my brother and I were taken out by two local fishermen who kept their boat on the beach by the cottage. I hung over the side as far as I dared and, for the first time, understood why people sometimes describe the sea as being like liquid glass. I had an uninterrupted view to the sea bottom, more than twenty feet down. I wanted to slide in. Not possible, for I was still trying to learn to swim and had spent the first two weeks of the holiday splashing about uselessly and drinking many mouthfuls of seawater. Just why did I keep sinking? It may have had something to do with the fact that previous to this day we had been trying to learn to swim in a lashing tide. Surfing would have been a better sport.

Unbelievably, we were on a beach holiday for the whole of July 1968. How did my parents manage that? Thinking back, my dad had lodged in Kilkeel for his work earlier that year and must have met someone there who put him on to the wee house on Ballymartin beach. Holidays before that had been in a caravan for the Twelfth fortnight in Bunny's Caravan Park in Newcastle. Wonderful too, but not as spectacular as being in a beach cottage for a whole month in a part of coastal Northern Ireland where the Mourne Mountains meet the sea, which I loved – and love so much that I now live just around the coast in Rostrevor.

My mother and I going for a swim from the cottage in Ballymartin.

The day out in the boat was the first and only still day we experienced during our four-week holiday – and we didn't even get a chance to swim. Instead I had to be content with trailing my hand in the water as the two fishermen rowed out far away from our holiday cottage and then stopped to drop mackerel feathers (fishing lures) down into the water. They knew where to stop for mackerel that came in like a storm chasing shoals of sand eels. The shoals I saw that day were as big as cars, and flashed and glinted like highly polished silver. They sped through the water, twisting, turning then splitting up into smaller shoals as their hungry enemy the mackerel went after them. Mackerel are even more magnificent in appearance than slick little sand eels. Their metallic scales range from blue to blue-green then somehow or other into coral pink with a silver trim. Go and see these beauties in County Down's Exploris Aquarium. You will wonder why anyone wants to catch these magical fish and eat them – but I do, for they are as delicious cooked as they are to look at.

Imagine being in that little rowing boat, watching from overhead as the drama unfolds below. The mackerel chase the sand eel shoals close into the tide line until they run out of water, then the eels must back-flip to try and get back out to sea. Sadly, they back-flip into the mouths of the mackerel. The sea boils like a saucepan of water waiting for pasta, and you can hear slapping and snapping sounds in the battle between the mackerel and doomed eels.

We were given a bucket of mackerel by the fishermen that day when we got back to shore. I could see mixed looks on my family's faces. They appreciated the kindness of the fishermen in taking me and my brother out (we were no bother really – we didn't utter a word as we were both so hypnotised by the wonderful experience) – and the gift of mackerel, but for goodness' sake what were we going to do with the fish? Living in the middle of Tyrone, far away from the sea, we never ate mackerel as it goes off almost immediately unless it is iced and refrigerated

The giving of gifts of food during times of surplus is part of our culture. It is inherent in us to share and appreciate, and to be kind to our neighbours. It is dishonourable to show anything other than appreciation, so my mother thanked the fishermen very much then waved them off.

'Keep them in the cold sea water until you are ready to cook them, and you need to use them in the next couple of hours,' shouted one of the fishermen over his shoulder as he headed for the lane leading up to the main road. He left as fast as a sand eel.

'How do I cook them?' shouted my mother, but he was gone.

'What now?' I asked.

Family meeting, of course. We all sat round the table – my mother, my granny, my Aunt Lynn and me, all of whom knew nothing about cooking oily fish that was likely to go off before we stopped arguing about what to do with it.

Our little cottage on the shoreline faced the sea. We kept the front door open all day until we went to bed at night. The front door opened right into the living room, where the table sat in the middle of the room, watching the tide come and go twice a day. There was a gas cooker, a couple of shelves and a Belfast sink with a wooden drainer. Two enamel buckets stood guard beside the sink for there was no running water. If I wanted a drink,

I dipped into the cool, clear, delicious water that we got from the well at the bottom of the lane. Facing each other across this room were the bedroom doors, with a variety of beds. There were washed-out pink floral-patterned curtains that barely kept the light out, but I didn't mind, for I was happy to leap out of bed in the morning as soon as I was allowed and go straight to the sea to practise swimming. And the most restful, sleep-inducing sound is that of the tide a few yards from your door. I lay in bed every night listening to all its different movements: dancing, splashing, thumping against the rocky beach and sometimes even cheekily splashing the front windows. On this mackerel day it slid in over the sand and rocks like a creeping cat silently pursuing her prey. Had it been its usual choppy self, I doubt that I would have accepted the invitation earlier on in the day to go in the boat.

Nanny Wylie put the teapot in the middle of the table and Aunt Lynn put out a plateful of arrowroot biscuits, saying, 'These are your granny's. You'll have to run up to the shop and get more before bedtime.'

We began dipping our biscuits in the tea then washed them down with satisfied slurps. Quickly my siblings finished and ran off to play on the beach. I stayed my ground for the cookery debate.

Nanny Wylie began. 'You can just fry them on the pan.'

'Not on my good frying pan!' came my mother's reply. She had brought her own one from home because in holiday accommodation the pans provided were cheap and thin, and usually burned. 'I don't want the stink of the fish in the house either.'

'Sure they're fresh – fresh fish don't be smelly,' said Nanny Wylie.

'What about a barbecue?' said my mother, ever adventurous.

The debate rumbled on. I wanted to join in and say, 'Are we going to get anything to eat tonight?' But then I would have become the problem, so I said instead, 'I'm starving.'

'Run up to the shop and buy more arrowroot biscuits,' said my mother, 'and hurry up. Is there enough water? You might have to go to the well.' My mother got her purse out and thought for a moment before saying, 'And see if there's any tinfoil in that shop' – the nearest one, a very steep climb – 'and if they don't have any then go to the other one.'

'What? The one halfway up the mountain?'

'Don't be silly – the one on the Annalong Road.'

'What's the tinfoil for?' asked Aunt Lynn.

'Mind your own business,' said my mother, then, to me, 'You can do the spuds when you get back.'

I took the coins and shopping bag from my mother and, in a hurry, running out the door to get on with whatever it took to get the dinner on the table, I nearly collided with my grandmother, who was striding outside with the determination of someone with a plan. We paused at the white enamel bucket sitting at the front door, full of dead mackerel and seawater.

I asked, 'Will they keep?'

She answered, 'Yes, if you hurry up.'

I began the steep ascent to Ballymartin village. The

lane was a single-person track from the beach up to the main road. It zigzagged a fair bit to compensate for the steepness. At the top was a little lay-by where, when we'd arrived, my dad had parked the car and we had made relays with luggage, bedding, just-in-case cooking equipment and a carton of groceries. I had been charged with carrying a stone-weight bag of potatoes. We must have looked like Mongolian nomads carting our belongings down to the shore then dumping them all in front of the cottage while there was a momentary panic about the key. I tried carrying the bag of potatoes on my head as I had seen tribal women do in pictures in my geography book at school. Not a good idea on a steep slope – a couple of times I slipped and landed on my backside. This was out of my comfort zone.

My mother carried a suitcase in each hand and Dad, on this first trip, took the box of groceries. My brother carried his football and my sister a little vanity case she had got for Christmas, full of beads, pretend earrings and hair slides. We all kept our heads down and concentrated on not slipping. I expect my parents were worrying that they'd made a mistake in booking this cottage for a month. They knew there was no running water or electricity – this was no big deal as many of our rural relatives in the 1960s still lived this way. It was the awfulness of that near-vertical track that weighed on their minds. However, they didn't worry for long. As soon as my dad had found the key, opened up and got the gas cooker going, it was time for tea, and who was sent back up the lane to the village to look for a shop to get the milk? Me.

This initial outing for milk was a marker of how the rest of the holiday was going to go. The milkman left three pints in the lay-by for us every morning and I had to go and get it before it got too warm. Thank goodness the well was nearby.

The day we'd been out in the boat, as I started the climb up the lane, I knew full well that the little shop-cum-post-office wouldn't have foil. They stocked the bare necessities – a few tins, biscuits, potatoes, tea and sugar. The milk bottles sat in a crate on the floor and there was a small ice cream fridge for tourists and campers who stopped on their way to the big caravan sites further down the road in Cranfield. The shop was off the living room, like many of its time, with a bell on the door, so when someone arrived the two sisters who owned the shop were alerted. I usually saw them at their kitchen sink in the adjoining scullery washing dishes or peeling potatoes. The sisters had got to know us and liked to have a chat. There was often quite a wait before they arrived at the counter of the shop.

'Oh, how is your mummy and daddy?' asked Miss Shop.

'Daddy is still working this week – he only gets two weeks off but he is coming to stay this weekend. He's going to take us to Tollymore Forest.'

The conversation continued with the ladies enquiring after Nanny Wylie and Aunt Lynn, and giving plenty of advice about how my granny could treat her bunions. Finally they asked what I wanted. They were able to supply the arrowroot biscuits but – as I already knew

– they didn't have any tinfoil.

'You would have to go into Kilkeel for that. What does she want tinfoil for?'

'Not sure, but they told me not to come back without any. Might be something to do with the mackerel – I got out on a boat today with the fishermen.'

They both lit up and Miss Shop said, 'Oh, that will be Johnny and Eddie. They left us a couple of fish too. Listen, dear, go next door to Mrs Smith and say I sent you. She's always baking and she might have some tinfoil. That will be sixpence, please. Tell Mummy and all we were asking for them.'

Mrs Smith went over the same conversational ground with me and said, 'Yes, of course,' about the tinfoil. 'When your daddy is here next week you can get me a replacement roll in Kilkeel. You can drop it in.'

I ran down the track to the well, stopped and had a good slurp of water. Mission successful: arrowroot biscuits and tinfoil. I could smell smoke – Nanny Wylie had built a substantial bonfire out of driftwood on the beach just above the tide line. It whooshed and roared and threw sparks high above the roof of our little cottage into the thermal currents that lifted the sea birds high over the raised beach. My mother and Aunt Lynn were busy gutting the mackerel on the waist-height stone wall that bordered the patio, dropping each fillet into a bucket of cold well water.

When the fire was hot enough, Nanny Wylie made a flat area in the embers and neatly placed two potatoes for each of us in it. As time passed, I watched the potatoes blacken and asked if they were burnt. Nanny Wylie reassured me that they would be lovely and fluffy inside. Then my mother wrapped each fish in tinfoil and laid them in a row in another flattened area of embers. Within a couple of minutes, the contents of the foil began to sizzle and squeak.

Along the low wall were plates for everyone with a couple of scallions each, the butter dish, salt and glasses for milk. As Aunt Lynn doled out the fish Nanny Wylie followed with scooped-out potato, equally delicious looking. We all sat around the fire again on our rocks for the feast of mackerel, scallions and potatoes dripping with butter and crusted with salt, and savoured the experience.

Good fish cookery is dependent on two things: freshness and speed. Speed in this case means a high temperature. The reason I have such an intense memory of the Ballymartin mackerel is because all these key factors came together. Another reason that this meal was so delicious was the quality of the potatoes grown in the area. Everyone in this end of County Down still eagerly awaits the arrival of floury potatoes around the middle of July. Many farms still sell them out of their barns, freshly dug, not sealed in a plastic bag, for this will suffocate and sweat them. If it's plastic it will be left open for the potatoes to breathe. Paper is better – bring your own bag and save the planet while you are at it.

Make friends with a fisherman who can supply the mackerel or take up mackerel fishing yourself. Bring your barbecue to the beach – all food tastes better outside anyway. Mustard is the perfect accompaniment for the mackerel. Soda or wheaten bread provide starch and a salad on the side with onions is good. Onions help cut the oiliness of the fish. An old tin teapot to make a brew on the bonfire or barbecue will round everything off nicely.

Wheaten Bread

4oz (100g) sieved plain flour
12oz (300g) medium wholemeal flour
1 tsp salt
1 tsp baking soda (bicarbonate of soda)
1oz (25g) butter
buttermilk, about ¾ pint (375ml)

Grease a 9 inch (23cm) cake tin with oil or butter and sprinkle it with flour.

Heat your oven to 220°C.

Put all the ingredients except the buttermilk into a mixer and pulse until the mixture looks like breadcrumbs. Add enough buttermilk to bind everything together into a light, springy dough. Try not to overmix it or your bread will be tough.

Transfer the mixture into the prepared loaf tin and bake for around 45 minutes. The way to find out if the bread is cooked is to pierce it with a skewer. The skewer should come out clean.

Turn the bread out onto a cooling tray and cover with a clean tea towel.

9

Domestic Science

Breakfast menu from my school recipe book

I can't spell. Worse than that, looking over my school recipe book, I realise that I am still not confident spelling the words that tripped me up as a child. There they are, all lined up in my eleven-year-old writing: grapfriut, sasage, tamoto and on later pages, patoto, and on the cover, Recipies. As you can see, my teacher only indicated one spelling mistake. She was the domestic science teacher, so she may have felt spelling was the English teacher's job. I still look at this page with wonderment but reassure myself that even though I was lazy and had neglected my spellings, I had never needed to write some of these words down until domestic science in 1967.

Were we being taught breakfast had two courses? Really? I am sure no one questioned this at the time – we were just glad to be allowed near some food, at last. In our domestic science lessons the first meanness we were to experience was being forced to make an over-complicated apron. We weren't allowed to start cooking until it was completed, and the whole class was held to ransom while we struggled with this task. The apron was the kind of thing you would see in 1950s American advertisements aimed at housewives who, if you believed the hype, had waists like wasps, never a hair out of place, and somehow or other managed the daily grind in the kitchen with a smile and wearing high heels.

The offending garment consisted of a gathered knee-length half-skirt attached to a bib. The bib was strapped on by two crossover shoulder straps and secured at the back by a band that went round our waists and then tied. This engineering project required perfectly sewn ninety-degree corners and the ability to turn all of the straps inside out whilst they behaved like a barrel of snakes, the rule being the inside of the garment should look as good as the outside.

We were not required to wear the scarf shown on the picture on the front of the apron pattern, but we were berated if our hair was not either tied up or held back with a hair band. There were many scoldings about long nails and nail varnish from the domestic science teachers. It was their job also to check the length of our gym slips and to serve out punishments to those girls whose slips were too short. So here was I, in 1967, finally the right age for the cookery classes I had been looking forward to more than any other, only to find that they were run as an oppressive sexist regime by women, who were answerable to the men who had decided that girls should do cookery and not science. I survived because I loved food and cooking so much. Fifty years later, one of my friends still feels sick every time she walks past the school because of her bad experiences in the domestic science room. We stuck it out that first year from September until nearly Easter, when all our aprons were finally finished and fit to be worn, and finally we were allowed to cook.

I was happier now. I was finally going to find out how to make soda bread like Nanny Wylie but this time with a recipe that I would be able to follow. Her farls were thinner and softer than we have today, so they slipped down like honey. Our domestic science efforts, of course, were burnt, tough, doughy, or all three. We were made to eat half a buttered soda farl in front of the teacher, who watched us very carefully to make sure none went into any gymslip pocket. She need not have worried – we were totally conditioned to do what we were told and would never have dreamed of wasting food. The rest of the soda farls we took home for our families. The teacher making us eat burnt doughy bread was a way of making us think, 'If I had listened better and done what I was told instead of talking to Mary, then I would not be suffering right now.' Well, we verbalised our feelings about the teacher outside in the playground later: 'Witch'.

Many people back then still relied on a traditional range fuelled by coal, turf or logs for cooking. Not us town girls, though: even if our rural relatives still used them, to us the stove was a source of comfort looked after by people wiser and more capable than ourselves. These black cast-iron dragons breathed smoke, fire and fear – we were all used to plenty of jobs at home, but stoking a stove was not one of them. The domestic science room was possessed of one of these beasts. We only ever used it once. I guess it was an item on the curriculum that the inspector asked about when he came. Correct use of a griddle, maintaining an even temperature on a cantankerous old range and working with sticky, runny dough are challenges in themselves, without the added anxiety of being right beside the desk of a teacher who looked on with the expression of a crow about to tackle some roadkill. When my turn came to coax the beast to the right temperature and produce four perfect pancakes, I was shaking with fear and sweating. The blasted thing was getting cold and my pancakes were not getting brown.

'Put in some coke, you silly girl,' roared the teacher when I dared to mention my problem.

No one had showed us how so I had no idea what to do. This catering range was much more complicated than anything I had seen before. There was a door into the fire box with metal handles and an oven glove with a hole burnt in the middle to hold the scorching handle. Don't think so, Miss, I said to myself.

'Please miss, where do I get the coke? This bucket is empty.'

'For goodness' sake,' she said, running into the other domestic science teacher's classroom. 'Miss Wolf, did the caretaker not know to bring extra coke today?'

Miss Wolf looked up from her sewing and shrugged her shoulders.

Apparently the coke was finished so I was saved the torture, and instructed instead to take the griddle away from the stove and cook my pancakes on an ordinary cooker. Hallelujah. I was the last girl and the others had sweated through griddling fruit scones, fruit sodas, treacle farls and soda farls. The smell was great; the reward was the divinely soft butter-drenched warm griddle breads. We were sweaty and exhausted from fear, but we had reproduced the smells, tastes, and food of our mothers' and grandmothers' kitchens. We were transported from hell to heaven above; the dragon stove was forgiven; even the crow teacher smiled in the end.

We copied all the recipes for these griddled breads from Margaret Bates' *The Belfast Cookery Book*. They are recipes I still use today. The copies of the precious book, hardback and expensive, were counted out at the start of the class and counted back in again at the end. Even today the book is much sought after and valued. Margaret Bates states in the chapter on Bread, Cakes and Biscuits that 'Ulster's heritage in the matter of bread, cakes and biscuits is considerable, for her housewives delight in a well-laden tea table … Pride of place must go to soda bread with its floury, brown crossed crust, spongy farls fresh from the griddle.' As an eleven-year-old child I couldn't disagree with this statement – my life experience so far had confirmed it. It took me a while longer to figure out that I was being trained to be a good housewife.

Nanny Wylie understood my love of food and gave me a copy of *The Modern Family Cookbook* by the American author Meta Given. This was the textbook that my aunt had used for her tech cookery course. As part of Meta's 'Meal Planner's Creed', she states, 'My family's health, security, and pleasure depend on my skill in planning meals.' Wow, Meta, that's a big responsibility. She outstrips Margaret Bates with 60 bread recipes, 40 cake recipes and 120 cookie recipes. Of course, I wanted to try them all, but that amount of baking is a lifetime's work. I have done my best whenever I have had the chance over the years: home-made doughnuts for a three-hundred-bed hospital where I worked as a chef briefly; home-made pancakes on Shrove Tuesday for a hundred residents in a hostel for the homeless; and, of course, I make home-made bread for any party or visitors.

At school, before we were allowed to progress to cakes or biscuits, we were expected to acquire the ability to make a good broth, a brown stew and proper brown gravy, not the packet type. The brown stew I didn't get – it was canteen food only fit for school meals. We only ever got Irish Stew at home.

Everyone should be able to make Irish Stew, a comforting, nutritious meal that is easily prepared. It's well worth a bit of bother peeling vegetables and since you are at the sink, why not make a really big pot with enough stew for two days? As it is a complete meal there is no need to prepare additional vegetables, and the flavour develops overnight; another good reason for having enough for more than one day. It's good I think to have some sort of stew or soup on top of the cooker, for you never know who will drop in. I'm sure this is how my ancestors thought of it. When I am planning to make stew, I make sure I have lamb shoulder chops in the freezer, or pork shoulder. These cuts are more flavoursome and break down into flakes of meat and flavour. Leaner, more expensive cuts like chuck steak (also known as topside) will dry out and become tough.

The home cooking way of making this stew is to place your meat in the bottom of a large heavy pot with a little water and start cooking over a low heat. Next, add layers of peeled potatoes, carrots and onions – potatoes being the main ingredient. I normally use 5½lb (2½kg). Seasoning is ½ teaspoon white pepper, 1 teaspoon mustard powder and 1–2 teaspoons salt according to taste. Add water to about a third of the height of the pot, turn the heat way down low, cover with a tight-fitting lid and cook until the vegetables are soft, checking from time to time to make sure that the stew hasn't gone dry.

Thank goodness, after a bad start, we got on to the good stuff for the next three years. What I brought home from school was soon good enough to constitute a family meal and give my mother a night off. When we made Irish Stew in school, I was given a vital motto from Miss Carrion Crow: 'A stew boiled is a stew spoiled!' This is good advice – it's always best to keep any stew at a low simmer rather than a rolling boil. We also learnt about the cuts of meat and how to make the cheaper cuts (shin, topside and flank) tender by stewing. The tasty meat juices that escape during cooking are preserved in the cooking liquid. This is why soups and stews made with these cuts are so good.

There are really important basics involved in making good pastry that I learned at school and that are seared on my brain forever. All pastries are fat, flour and water. The water must be ice cold. The oven must be at least moderately hot to hot depending on what you are making. The flour must be soft cake flour as it absorbs the fat and will not produce a tough paste. The fat should ideally be 50 per cent lard and 50 per cent butter. Forget about margarine – the plant oils in it melt very quickly and make the pastry soggy. Lard does not melt so quickly and therefore gives a wonderful biscuity crust. The final trick for any pastry is to rest it in the fridge for a couple of hours before you use it. It is easier to handle and it cooks better.

I happily cooked my way through shortcrust pastry (apple tart), flaky pastry (steak and kidney pie), rough puff pastry (Russian fish pie). By the age of thirteen I could quote the standard recipes for all of these types of pastry. This stood me in good stead because we were examined about pastry: we had to be able to reproduce the ingredients, method and principles of pastry making from memory. I did because I loved it. I scored the highest domestic science marks in third year in the whole school despite being harangued in just about every single domestic science lesson by Miss Carrion Crow. I was not alone – we all got worn down because it was clear that the teacher didn't see any potential or ability in us.

The worst time of year was before the school speech days when we were required, as future hostesses and housewives, to make the supper for the whole school as well as visiting parents, governors and guests. There was cooking and crying all day. My friend Carol was tasked with making an entire loaf of ham sandwiches. The correct way to do this, according to the teachers, was to stack the loaf of sandwiches up like a tower, then cut off all the crusts with a very long bread knife.

'MAKE SURE THERE IS NO CRUST WHATSOEVER ON THOSE SANDWICHES,' shrieked the crow.

What would happen? Would we be caned? Would there be lines? Would the principal lose his job if the chair of the board of governors found a millimetre of brown crust on his otherwise white bread ham sandwich? Would we all remain single as no man would marry a girl who could not cleanly slice the crusts off an entire loaf of ham sandwiches in one smooth stroke?

So Carol stood in the shadow of a pan loaf that had doubled in size with its fillings (the filling had to be as thick as a single slice of bread or you would fail your domestic science O level). Planted on the stainless steel work bench on a bread board, the sandwich tower was taller than Carol was. She stood there in her complicated blue apron, sewn up under the dictatorship of the crow, with a thirty-inch-long bread knife, trying to maintain her composure. I could see she was considering her options. Every girl in the classroom was silent. We were all considering our options. My preferred one was finding an excuse to hide in the larder. Others were considering leaving the country, I'm sure. But we were frozen to the spot and none of us could help, for if we had we would've been punished. Eventually, Carol went for it. Of course the loaf tower began to topple and the sandwiches began to come apart.

'PRESS DOWN ON THE BREAD,' came the next squawk.

However, Carol couldn't reach the top of the sandwich tower. She put the knife down on the table and as the tears became a river she took a freshly laundered and pressed cotton hankie out of her pocket and mopped her eyes.

'YOU STUPID GIRL!'

Crow winged it down the classroom. Like an experienced executioner she cleanly removed the crusts then sliced the pile into four triangles.

'Go and get the sandwich plates,' she yelled at no one in particular. We scattered to the store cupboard, sweeping up Carol and patting her on the back. She stayed there while the rest of us divided the sandwiches out between the plates. We were instructed to cover everything with greaseproof paper and then with damp linen tea towels, and then it was time to go. The later classes would set up the supper in the domestic science rooms for the guests.

On the evening in question we all filtered down from the assembly hall after the speech day was finished. We were shocked by the smile on the crow's face, then watched her cautiously as she sipped tea from a china cup, chatting pleasantly to those people she felt were important. Some of the mothers could not face coming as far as the domestic science rooms – they did not want to return to the site where they were tortured as schoolgirls. Nothing had changed, but they had all managed to get married and nourish their families.

I took my parents for their supper – I had made sausage pinwheels and wanted to show off. Sausage pinwheels are made with puff pastry rolled around seasoned sausage meat and baked in slices. But I did not eat any ham sandwiches. Carol and her mother also went to the domestic science room. Standing near the ham sandwiches they held hands very tightly. Carol's mum gave the crow a long look, put her arm around Carol's shoulder then left, sweeping past her like the Queen Mother sheltering Princess Elizabeth.

This was our final year at secondary school – depending on exam results we would progress now either to the grammar school or to technical college. Either way we were all now rid of the torture of this regime.

Russian Fish Pie

Before I give you the recipe, the obvious question is what has Russian Fish Pie got to do with a Northern Irish food inheritance? I believe it may be the Northern Ireland nod to the Russian *kulebyaka* (or *coulibiac*) fish pie – a wonder in its own right and definitely worth making. Margaret Bates includes it in her chapter on 'Foreign Food' in *The Belfast Cookery Book*. The best thing about this recipe is that you use the cooking liquor from the fish to make the white sauce that binds it all together.

White sauce featured widely in the 1960s Northern Irish diet. It felt like no meal was complete without it – parsley sauce for fish, mustard sauce for boiled ham, gravy made with flour. Even Christmas didn't escape – brandy sauce was just white sauce with brandy. How did this pasty world come about? During a later cookery qualification I discovered that the standard catering text book, *Practical Cookery* by Victor Ceserani MBE and Ronald Kinton, is full of the stuff. Not sure whether to blame the French (who call it béchamel) or the Italians for this widespread use of something that can also be used for wallpaper paste, but my English mother-in-law bought into it. When faced with a new exotic vegetable, say kohlrabi, she would boil it, cover it in white sauce and finish it off in the oven.

She often threw in a teaspoon of mustard, the only thing that rescues this dreaded sauce, the end result of which is a mush which you can't quite identify, but doesn't offend too much – so you can eat it whilst listening to the story about the neighbour's allotment and all the new vegetables he has introduced. The addition of cheese, a good strong one, also helps, and if you are boiling vegetables, use the cooking liquid as well as the milk in the sauce, so you might at least get a hint of what the vegetable tastes like.

Margaret Bates advises this in the *Belfast Cookery Book,* then goes on to give us all the variations, including a velouté, a hybrid of white sauce that is more involved but, in my opinion, by far the best way to include a flour-based sauce in the kitchen. I prefer cornflour to flour – it is lighter, is less likely to go lumpy, and cooks quicker. It is also gluten-free.

In the 'Foreign Food' chapter of the Bates book there is a good range of continental and curry recipes, demonstrating, I suppose, lifestyle shifts and reflecting the foreign holidays that were now a possibility for some of the population. Of course any sixties foodie who got to sample continental exotica like this would want to share it. The worst example I came across was Mars bar sandwiches – perhaps a translation of pain au chocolat. The best example is Russian Fish Pie. If I ever had the opportunity I would like to invite a foodie Russian round to show me how to make a real *kulebyaka*.

Rough Puff pastry
8oz (200g) sieved plain flour
pinch of salt
6oz (150g) butter at room temperature
¼ pint (125ml) ice-cold water

Sieve the flour and salt together. Cut the butter into small pieces and lightly mix them into the flour without rubbing in. Make a well in the centre of the mixture and pour in the water. Mix to a stiff dough.

Turn the pastry out on to a floured surface and roll it out into an oblong strip approximately 12×4 inches (30×10cm), keeping the sides straight and the corners square. Fold it in half, turn it 90 degrees and roll out to the same size as before. Repeat this process once more.

Cover with cling film and let the pastry rest in the

fridge until quite cool. Making it the day before is a good strategy.

Filling
1lb fish (400g), a mix of white and smoked is good;
   you can also throw in a few prawns
½ pint (300ml) milk, plus a little extra
salt and white pepper
fresh parsley, chopped, about a teaspoonful
½ tbsp cornflour
2 hard-boiled eggs
2 vine tomatoes, skinned
1 egg, beaten

Cook the fish in the seasoned milk until it is just loosening up – this usually takes about five minutes. You need to watch it – it could take less time, and if the fish goes hard it is ruined. Remove it with a slotted spoon, set it aside to cool. Add the chopped parsley to the milk.

Blend the cornflour with a small amount of cold milk and gradually stir into the milk in the saucepan, heating gently. Keep stirring until the cornflour thickens the sauce. Remove from the heat. Break the fish into chunks and gently add to the sauce. This filling should be quite thick but not solid – add a little more milk if necessary. Taste to check the seasoning. Allow the filling to cool before you assemble the pie.

When you are ready, heat the oven to 200°C. On a floured surface, roll out the pastry into a large square ½cm thick. Lightly dust a baking tray with flour. Lay the pastry on the tray, then in the middle of it place the fish filling. Cover the filling with slices of hard-boiled eggs and tomatoes. Brush the edges of the pastry with the beaten egg and fold in the four corners, like an envelope. Brush the entire package with egg. If you want something a bit more fancy, shape the remaining scraps of pastry into leaves for decoration. Use the egg to attach them to the envelope and don't forget to brush the leaves with more egg. Bake in the oven for approximately 45 minutes. This is as good cold as it is hot.

10

Flower Power and *An Invitation to Indian Cooking*

In 1970 I graduated to grammar school to take O levels and, if I worked hard enough, A levels, then university. Since domestic science and art were my best subjects I chose these along with the compulsory ones. I was fourteen. I could make with confidence all sorts of pastry and was responsible for one meal per week at home. The expectations were high – spuds and butter with cabbage and bacon were still on the menu, but on my night everyone sat promptly at the table with eyes like saucers. Even the dog presented herself early – her scraps had got more interesting. I got the go-ahead from my mother for a budget and would scour the town for things like the Worcester sauce that was given in my domestic science cookery book as an ingredient in the liver gravy and bacon. I used the new alchemy I was learning at school to introduce some new food ideas at home.

Worcester sauce really works with liver. Offal was standard fare in the 70s. When we got liver and bacon at school, there were no leftovers. This may have been because a teacher sat at the head of each dinner table and made sure we ate everything, or it could have been because we were hungry enough to eat anything. And it was definitely the case that the dinner ladies cooked the liver really well. There was good thick gravy full of onions made from the cooking liquor, the accompanying bacon was always crisp and the creamed potatoes soaked up the gravy. Choice was not on the menu until many years later and, as I had never been to a restaurant or cafe, I did not really understand the concept. My only choice regarding food came on the one night that I was allowed to cook. I loved heading off to the delicatessen aisles of Irwin's Grocery in Woodhouse Street, Portadown.

I always knew what I was going to make and had my list of ingredients with me. My freedom did not extend to random purchases, but these outings definitely did give me the opportunity to closely examine ingredients I was not familiar with, and gave me ideas for future meals. Worcester sauce was interesting enough for now – included in its ingredients were both tamarinds and anchovies. I found a bottle no problem – Irwin's had quite an exotic range of accompaniments and relishes, and there was a wonderful aroma of roasting coffee. ('Surely to God coffee comes out of a Camp bottle,' said my aunt when I mentioned it to her.) The same aunt once broke out and bought Thousand Island dressing, which we tried and quite liked, but the purchase was a one-off. It was enjoyable enough, though, to stay in my food mind, and I still use the recipe from *The Modern Family Cookbook* by Meta Given. It's basically mayonnaise with chopped red pepper, gherkins, and hard-boiled egg, and a good squeeze of lemon. Great with fish.

The night I was cooking liver and bacon I felt confident about what I was doing – liver and bacon was a regular family meal, and Dad especially was keen on flavoursome food. I had everything laid out on the kitchen table – there were no worktops then – in the way that I'd been taught at school. There was a plate of seasoned flour to coat the liver, as well as onions, chopped parsley and the Worcester sauce. My mother had peeled the spuds and they were now boiling merrily on the stove. She had just put on a saucepan of cabbage to boil next to the spuds and was about to add a pinch of baking soda.

'Mummy, the teacher said not to add baking soda to cabbage because it destroys the vitamin C.'

Domestic science had made me fixated on vitamin C. If you peel too much potato off your spuds with the skin, then the vitamin C is gone – it is just under the surface of the skin. If you use old vegetables the vitamin C has perished. God forbid my mother would put baking soda in boiled cabbage as she had done all her life … somehow we survived and did not suffer from scurvy. Actually, adding a pinch of baking soda to the water produces a light purée of cabbage leaves, once they are cooked and well drained. Giving the cabbage a quick sauté in bacon fat makes a delicious side dish. As I coated the washed pig's liver in seasoned flour my mother was melting the bacon fat from the pan and was pouring it into an old china cup she kept for the purpose.

'Mummy, leave some of that fat on the pan, please. I'm nearly ready to cook the liver.'

The meal was well received – it was always a good sign

when there was a request for bread to mop up the gravy. I asked my father if he knew what tamarinds were – I wondered if he'd ever come across them when he was in the RAF. 'Joni in the health food shop says they're from India.' 'Is Joni that girl that wears those hippy clothes?' asked my mother.

End of conversation. Hippy was a dirty word – hippies definitely didn't get a good press in the *News of the World*, my dad's favourite paper.

As well as Irwin's, the new health food shop was a favourite place of mine. Joni was a vegetarian, and my friends and I hung around this new exotic location in Portadown, finding out more about hippies, and what Joni ate.

Joni didn't look like anyone else I knew. She wore long skirts, Jesus sandals and had strawberry-blonde hair down to her waist. Over her official-looking white coat, she wore several lengths of love beads and sported carefully applied kohl eyeliner. This turned out to come in a small thin black box that had a picture of a very beautiful Indian girl and the Taj Mahal on the front. Make-up in a food shop?

'Most make-up is tested on animals – they squirt shampoo into rabbits' eyes and things like that to find out if it's safe for humans. This kohl is cruelty free,' she told us. Right enough, I didn't like the sound of testing on animals – and I decided that I wouldn't tell her that I'd had rabbit stew for lunch the week before at my grandmother's.

'What do you eat instead of meat?' I asked her. She enthusiastically sold me the idea that soya beans were a wonderful meat substitute in stews and worked particularly well as they had similar proteins to meat. I bought some with my pocket money as they were so cheap, with the intention of trying them at a later date.

'How do I cook these? What do they taste like?' I asked

'Oh, quite nice. You have to soak them overnight in water and then boil them for an hour and a half. You could put some soy sauce on them.'

I thought about this. 'What about Worcester sauce?'

'Well, that's not really vegetarian because there are anchovies in it.'

She invited us round to her flat the next afternoon after school – it was her day off – to try soya bean stew.

Her flatmate Roxanne answered the door. Joni was busy watering her overgrown spider plants in a haze of smoke. There was a very strange mix of smells – perfume and something like beans cooking with Worcester sauce.

'Hiya, just going to make some tea. Would you like some?'

'Hiya Joni,' we said in turn. And yes we would like tea as we were parched. We had walked the two miles from school so we could keep our bus fare to spend on ourselves.

In the kitchen, Joni explained to me that Roxanne was on a macrobiotic diet. I found out later that there are no potatoes in a macrobiotic diet – too acidic; apparently they mess up your ying and yang. No potatoes? That would never do.

Joni spooned something on to a small plate for me

to taste. It looked like Irish Stew without the potatoes or meat, and with soya beans in it. I tried some and it was delicious. Roxanne explained that that was probably thanks to the miso, fermented soya bean paste.

Joni asked, 'What sort of tea would you like? Lapsang Souchong or Earl Grey?'

'What are those?'

'Lapsang Souchong is a perfumed China tea with a smoky flavour. Earl Grey is perfumed as well. I keep them in the health food shop and get staff discount.'

I decided to make the best of the unexpected sensory adventure and went for the China tea. Joni put a few leaves in the bottom of a bowl-shaped cup and filled it with boiling water.

We sat down on a low couch with the others and Joni handed me her and Roxanne's favourite recipe book, *Laurel's Kitchen*, to look at. I was fascinated by its claim that eating no meat could save the planet. That was good enough for me on one level – but on another level the food had to taste good too, so I wasn't planning on giving up bacon any time soon.

Little did I know that just around the corner was the 1974 Ulster Workers' Council Strike. It came about in the middle of our exams, in May. As I did my usual tour of the shops on the way home, I noticed the shelves getting empty. Next thing, the shops began to shut at odd times. I did listen to the local news and knew something was up but I had no idea of the gravity of the situation. Then one morning the electric went off and the milkman did not come. I walked to school with my friends as usual, for even though our electric was off it didn't mean the school electric was off. On the way, we noticed that it was strangely quiet and as we approached the school building there wasn't the usual queue of buses.

Out of curiosity, we went on up to the school door where a notice said that the school was closed. We could officially go home. When I got back to the house I found my dad back from work. The roads were blocked around the perimeter of the town. The manager at his depot had wisely decided to keep Post Office lorries off the road that day. We all sat at home looking at each other and feeling hungry.

'We'll go up to Aunty Sissy and get some goats' milk,' said Mummy helpfully.

'Sure the roads are blocked, we'll get nowhere,' replied Dad, 'and you wouldn't know what sort of carry-on there might be.'

'I'll run down to the shop and see is there any milk there,' I offered.

Most of the other kids in the estate had made the same offer. Not because we wanted to run messages; more because we wanted to witness this thing called a Workers' Strike. None of our parents seemed the slightest bit worried about sending us to the nearest shop. It was the duty of a sixties youngster to forage for food.

When I got to the shop, there were so many of us pushing and shoving that I could hardly get in the door. The bread shelves were empty and the milk fridge was empty. I grabbed a tin of Marvel and a tin of condensed milk and, as I was paying, the shop lights were switched off and the customers were clearing like snow off a ditch. When I stepped outside, the shop door slammed behind me and I could hear it being bolted.

Two army Land Rovers tore up the road with soldiers hanging out the back looking at us through the sights of their guns. We kids all froze and waited till they'd gone. Then, following a herd instinct, we turned the corner into the park entrance, which was adjacent to the shop, and ran like young deer to the top entrance of the park which was opposite our estate. We knew we could hide behind the high wall until everything looked safe. The gates were locked so the Land Rovers couldn't get in to us. When everything went quiet we just went over the wall, ran across the road and scattered to our houses.

This was new – we had never seen Land Rovers before with squaddies and rifles. In the beginning, my inclination was simply to gawk. In the end, it wasn't so much the army we were nervous about as the reaction of the local population who did not want this level of surveillance. It would have been easy to get drawn into stone throwing, or worse. At an early stage in my life, aged eleven, I'd decided I was not part of this argument and set about minding my own business, and being friends with people I liked, no matter what their background. It was also the love and peace era and this movement had much more appeal to me.

When I finally got back home, there was an old tin teapot boiling over the coal fire. My mother popped in a couple of spoonfuls of tea as I mixed the Marvel, 3½ tablespoons to one pint of water. My dad had found an old toasting fork in the shed so we had tea and toasted soda bread for lunch with butter and jam; there was always plenty of butter and jam.

My parents chatted. They had listened to the news on the radio and my dad decided he would go and get a hundredweight (a hundred pounds) of potatoes when the roadblocks were lifted. My mother decided she could fry stuff on the frying pan over the coal fire. And said she would make a ton of soda bread when the electric came back on. Soda bread will 'keep' for a couple of days in a bread bin. The best way to enjoy older bread is to fry it in bacon fat – this is delicious.

She did make a mountain of soda bread, and my dad did a rat run between barricades and army checkpoints for the potatoes. We had enough spuds to last us through the strike. We were holed up at home for the best part of two weeks. During this time the only way to find out if my scheduled exams were on or not was to walk to school in the morning and look at the notices on the door. The strike represented a troubling blackness that was beginning to stain the happy existence I had known until then. But in the main, I was preoccupied with my exams, ducking riots and being a teenager in hippydom.

The shops were never the same again because of the sectarian element that developed during the strike. People had been targeted and killed because they belonged to the Catholic community, or because they had to decided to carry on as normal and keep their business open, thus disobeying those leading the strike and paying for it with their lives. There was a palpable atmosphere of worry, and with good reason: people feared for their lives because of where they lived or what church building they went into on a Sunday morning.

There seemed to be more space around the goods on the shop shelves, and less of them. Who could blame the English and Irish suppliers for not wanting to send delivery vans full of goods to Northern Ireland? Would the stock be burnt? Would the vehicle be hijacked? Would the van be used to transport a bomb?

The old joy of meeting your neighbours in the grocery shops and spending a couple of hours yarning and joking became a thing of the past. Explosions and shots were common, as was the army roaring around the streets in their Land Rovers. I got an after-school job in Woolworths in Portadown. My favourite task was sitting on a stool at the entrance door to search everyone's bags in case they had a firebomb. What does a firebomb look like? I have no idea.

I ate my soda bread sausage sandwiches in the Woolworth's canteen at lunch time and thought about miso, imported from Japan. There were half a dozen packets on the shelf in the health food shop, and I wondered if I should buy one in case there was another strike. We always had spuds and it would make the stew taste good if there was no meat. Or I could buy a packet of TVP (textured vegetable protein made from soya beans, dried). It could be reconstituted as a mince substitute. I thought about the boring cake recipes in domestic science and the exciting save-the-world *Laurel's Kitchen* recipes. Could I save the world by becoming a vegetarian? It wouldn't save anybody in the Troubles but maybe it was a door with a chink of light coming through, a hippy world of love and peace on earth. I went through this door from time to time as an escape, for Northern Ireland was becoming very dark indeed.

I am not going to bore you with either soya bean stew or TVP shepherd's pie – those recipes are best left in the annals of the blackest days of the Troubles. My domestic science teacher at Portadown College trialled these ingredients at my behest, and the class tasted them. For those of us brought up on bacon as the main source of protein – and even for me who would try anything – this was just a step too far. The dishes tasted like chewed-up, spat-out and reconstituted carboard. Everyone in the class, with one exception, agreed. There were too many soya beans in *Laurel's Kitchen*, even if it was the vegetarian bible of the day. I did my best but there is nothing exciting or tasty about soy.

A good place of refuge for me turned out to be Madhur Jaffrey's *An Invitation to Indian Cooking* (1973). I had started babysitting for an Indian doctor from our local hospital and he made me dal for my lunch one day. Quick as porridge, aroma to die for, tasteful, economic and sustaining. Best of all, if there was any hint of a workers' strike, packets of red lentils were always last to go off the shelves. This recipe caught my imagination the minute the cumin seeds hit the hot oil; the resulting smell lifted me into heaven.

I was hooked on Indian food and, more specifically, on Indian vegetarian food. This has been part of the country's national heritage for hundreds of years and I would go as far as saying that you will not get better vegetarian food anywhere. I went to India and found out for myself in 1984. I did eventually become a vegetarian after saving up my bus money for Madhur Jaffrey's *Eastern Vegetarian Cooking*, the best place to start after tasting the dal, which turned out to be as good and homely as any Irish Stew.

Dal

4oz (100g) red lentils
½ tsp ground turmeric
2 tbsp vegetable oil
1 tsp cayenne pepper
8 whole cloves garlic
2 inch (6cm) stick cinnamon, flaked
½ tsp ground cumin
½ tsp cumin seeds
salt
pinch of sugar

Heat the oil in a heavy saucepan and fry all the ingredients except the salt and the sugar for a few seconds, no longer. The purpose of this exercise is to bring out the flavour of the spices and toast the lentils. You will know by the wonderful toasty aroma coming from the pan that you have achieved this. You can overdo this part and burn both the garlic and spices, making everything bitter. Now add about ½ pint water, a pinch of salt and a pinch of sugar, and turn the heat down to its lowest setting.

Cover the pot and leave to cook slowly until the lentils are soft, which usually takes about 10 to 15 minutes. Check occasionally and add small amounts of water if the lentils are sticking or burning. When it is cooked, it should have the consistency of thick porridge. Use the back of a spoon to crush the garlic. Stir the crushed garlic through the lentils.

Check the seasoning and serve with boiled rice (preferably basmati), yoghurt flavoured with mint, and tomato and onion salad.

The naan bread in the epilogue would make a great accompaniment, as would fried potato bread – it is Northern Ireland after all.

Epilogue

When I first discovered vegetarian food in Portadown, I could never have imagined that by 1980 I would be the chef at a vegetarian cafe in Belfast, located at the back of the Blackman's Tech on the ground floor of the old Mission for Seamen building. I had already spent several years cheffing in a variety of restaurants and kitchens. These jobs all involved turning out standard 1970s fare so the Rainbow Cafe was a dream job for me. I was now a fully-fledged vegetarian, believing I could save the world by not eating meat and promoting this lifestyle to anyone who expressed an interest. Besides, the food was wonderful – it seemed a natural progression from my wholesome homeplace eating. It nourished the soul and family as much as it nourished the body. My vegetarian and environmentally-minded friends debated the benefits of wholefood vegetarian cookery over vegetable curry just as much as my family had debated their food ideas over apple tart and soda bread. I felt I had arrived in the right place. Homeplace food was simple, easy to prepare, economic and comforting – so is good vegetarian food. Whatever food I cook and enjoy, I want to share it – this was what I said at my interview for the job.

The Rainbow Cafe was part of a project known as the Open College, an early movement to make education accessible to adults at a time when it was not in the least bit friendly to them. The cafe provided lunch for participants on the various courses in the college and opened its doors to anyone in Belfast at that time who either was a vegetarian or who would like to try the food. Upstairs, over the cafe, a group of artists had their studios. My American friend Karen had a pottery in the attic three floors up. I often used to take lunch up to her and another artist, Alice, a weaver, who dyed skeins of wool in boiled onion skins and many other wonderful vegetable sources.

From the beginning, Alice took me under her wing and gave me a copy of *The Cranks' Recipe Book*. Cranks was the original and best-known vegetarian restaurant in London. On my first day Alice and I sat down together at a long wood table in the canteen area of the Rainbow Cafe, went through the book and worked out the menu. I decided to make fresh bread every day. This was a real hit – the bread brought people in and then they tried the vegetarian cooking. A selection of salads, soups, and rice and bean dishes were available daily, as well as a selection of pastry items. I trialled many dishes that are common now but that were not available anywhere else in Northern Ireland at that time – hummus, tabbouleh, beansprouts and falafel, as well as pitta and naan bread. My County Armagh apple tart also became very popular; so did my friend Jack's vegan chocolate cake.

One afternoon I bumped into Karen as I was heading home. 'Listen,' said Karen. 'What about coming over on Saturday evening? We're going to have an Indian vegetarian meal. Jack's friend Ashok is cooking for us and I thought you would enjoy it.'

'Try and stop me. What time? What will I bring?'

'Come early if you want to see him do the prep, any time in the afternoon. Bring some of the naan bread you have on the menu.'

Naan bread reminds me of my grandmother's soda bread. Both are virtually instantaneous. You make a dough with plain flour, knead it lightly, then fire it onto a hot pan. It fluffs up like a miracle.

Some naan recipes require yeast, but this is not necessary, and this is where I see the similarity with soda bread. And a number of Indian breads, like Irish, use plain flours. This recipe is adapted from Madhur Jaffrey's *Eastern Vegetarian Cookery*.

Naan Bread

1lb (400g) plain flour (not strong flour)
1 tsp baking powder
1 tsp salt
1oz (25g) melted butter
1 pint (500ml) thin yoghurt
1 tsp cumin seeds, if you like

You will need a traditional griddle or a good heavy pan. Heat it up over a medium heat. If you sprinkle some flour on the surface of the pan and it starts to brown this is an indication it is at the correct temperature. Turn your grill to high.

Sift the flour, baking powder and a pinch of salt into a bowl. Then mix in the butter and yoghurt (and cumin seeds if using) until the dough starts to hold together. Turn out the dough on to a floured surface and knead well until it becomes smooth. Next divide the dough into eight pieces. Make each piece into a ball and roll it out with a rolling pin to a thickness of about an eighth of an inch. It doesn't need to be too neat in shape, just get it evenly thin in a sort of tear shape. Pop it onto the pan. It will need about five minutes there, then put the pan with the bread on it under the grill and within one to two minutes it will puff up. Once you see a few brown spots on the surface, you will know it is ready. Pile the naans on top of one another and cover with a clean tea towel. This will keep them warm enough until they are all cooked.

Hopefully you have a lovely friend like Ashok to share your bread with. On that Saturday night in Belfast, during the darkest days of the Troubles, he brought happiness to our little group of friends with his dal, spinach with paneer, lime pickle, cucumber and peanut salad and raita on the side. Dal is Indian comfort food and there are as many variations across their continent as there are here of Irish Stew.

Sitting around the fireplace after the meal, sipping China tea, staring into the glowing embers, a thought occurred to me: comfort food like mine and Ashok's, and the sharing of food, is what binds us all together.

Then I thought about Aunt Sarah, who was blind by then, over the lough in Tyrone, sitting in her cottage, listening to the radio. There would have been a knock at her back door earlier in the week and her weekly box of groceries would have been delivered straight to her kitchen table. She didn't need a phone – the order was the same every week.

The coal shed would be full; there would be a hundredweight of spuds in the barn, and carrots and beetroots buried in a pit to preserve them. There would be half a dozen different types of jam in the larder and half a dozen eggs left in by her neighbour yesterday. Milk would still arrive with her, and so would the mobile butcher. I hoped – believed – that in spite of the Troubles, life at home was going on as normal. People have to eat after all.

We all felt happy and contented on an island in time that night, safe with our full bellies, and prepared to sleep on the floor if we couldn't get home. Karen usually made omelette for breakfast. I was ready to move on from porridge anyway and interested to find out what Ashok's ideas on breakfast foods were. This felt like my new food family. Finding out how to make naan bread that was acceptable to Ashok was somehow a comfort for the loss of the soda bread prepared freshly every day by my grandmother. And to find friends like Karen and Jack, who sought out and savoured every food experience available to us then, was an unexpected joy, one that would sustain me for many years to come.

My stay at the Rainbow Cafe ended suddenly, when it ran out of money and had to close. Over the next few years, I juggled a family and a career in cooking. I had a lovely run of part-time jobs, including one in a vegetarian restaurant in Cyprus, but I eventually realised that babies and a cooking career weren't a good mix.

When my children became toddlers, I ran cookery courses and gave talks to groups and adult education classes. Then, I moved into teaching completely and became a lecturer in adult education. However, through all the twists and turns of my life, my love for cooking, and for sharing whatever I've made, has remained a constant. It's a great gift handed down to me from my food-loving family and one that I have been able to pass on to my own children and grandchildren.

My life still very much revolves around the making and sharing of food. Sometimes I bring a picnic to the shore for my swimming friends, sometimes I have friends around for lunch, or dinner. There is talk of a supper club among my foodie companions in Rostrevor, my adopted homeplace. It will happen in the near future, any excuse for cooking something traditional or experimental; this is what I do.

Acknowledgements

Where to start? The same place as the book, in the homeplace kitchen with my wonderful female relatives who passed on their love of food to me – my maternal grandmother Susan, my mother Heather and her sister Evelyn (Aunt Lynn). My life has been filled with foodie friends, with whom I have shared many, many excellent meals. Whether it was in Portadown where I started out or Rostrevor where I now live, Belinda, Ken and Sheila, Fil, Tom, my swimming buddies Heather and Victor – and everyone else who has had a meal in my house – became important tasters for my family recipes. I am grateful to all of you.

On the writing journey, Susannah Marriot and Helen Shipman, writing tutors in Falmouth University College, deserve special mention. So too do the team at Blackstaff Press who believed in my writing and made the book a reality; Helen, Patsy, Jenny and Jacky.